MW00414195

ALAN PLATT

FOREIGN
FOOL

Foolish Travel
Bangkok

FOREIGN FOOL

COPYRIGHT © ALAN PLATT 2015

All rights reserved.

This book or any portion thereof
may not be reproduced or used in any manner whatsoever
without the express written permission of the publisher,
except for the use of brief quotations in a book review.

Number One Bad has previously appeared in
Bald Ego, a New York literary and arts magazine.
Same Same appeared in Phuket Magazine.

Printed in the United States of America,
typeset in Garamond Pro, titles in Futura Medium,
book design and cover drawing by Alan Platt.

These are true stories, but names have been changed
and some locations have been disguised.

First Printing 2016

ISBN 978-616-394-416-0

Publisher
Foolish Travel
PASO Tower, Unit B, 25 Fl.,
88, Silhom Rd., Bangrak,
Bangkok 10500

www.foolishtravel.com

I am just a vagabond,
A drifter on the run,
And eloquent profanity
It rolls right off my tongue.

LOWELL GEORGE

Sometimes things went right.
But it's things going *wrong* that get the laughs
and the free drinks at the bar.

ALAN PLATT

INTRO

These travel disasters are all true. They all happened to me.
They're frank confessions of stupidity, embarrassment
and bumbling abroad, all written strictly for laughs,
although not all were quite so funny at the time.

For further dispatches from the same road movie,
to tell your own cringe-worthy travel tales,
or to meet others of the Wandering Class.
you might want to wander into here.
www.foreignfool.com

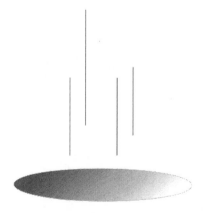

CONTENTS

NUMBER ONE BAD

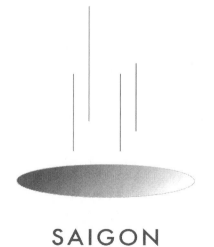

SAIGON

In Saigon, many years after the war was over, long after the city was declared safe for tourists and when even the hookers were becoming almost discreet, I was kidnapped.

That does sound a bit dramatic, I admit. Technically, it was more an abduction. But however one puts it, any mention of that sort of thing floods the mind with images of some poor guy being jumped by thugs, bundled into the trunk of a car and splattered across the tabloids with a screech of tires and the burning of rubber. None of that happened to me. I was kidnapped on a bicycle.

I should also add that the ruthless gang that pulled off this novel crime consisted of one rather frail old man. Which leaves us open to the inevitable question, of course. Who, in the ranks of the retarded, manages to get himself snatched on a bike? Well, there were a few extenuating circumstances. In such an unlikely scenario various key factors would have to present. In my own case these were - in no particular order - liquor, reefer and stupidity.

And the kidnap vehicle was not a regular bicycle, per se. That would make me a complete idiot, I grant you. It was a tricycle. But the point is that I was abducted on a pedaled vehicle by a doddering old man and here's how I did it. Or rather, here's how I was done.

Earlier that same afternoon I was not even there yet. I was still aloft in the rather over-friendly skies of Singapore Airlines, where 'final approach' refers to the last time the babes come around to fluff you.

I was preparing for my forthcoming adventure by enthusiastically embracing their "Let None Arrive Sober" policy. This entailed a certain amount of cooperation on my part in never refusing to have my wineglass refilled by an Asian centerfold. I could not say no, since I intended to propose marriage, or something briefer, to several of them before we entered Vietnamese airspace.

On Singapore Airlines the female help is apparently recruited by some kind of kabuki pornographer. The same specialist may also have designed the uniform, an ankle-length floral silk condom. And he surely must have had a hand in their famous ad campaign. You may remember it. It featured several of these sloe-eyed vamps batting their eyelashes at the camera and purring "I'm Singapore Airlines. Fly me." As Jack Nicholson once said, "Wrong *verb,* Honey."

It was hard to concentrate on the old guidebook. But I did manage to cast one bloodshot eye over the thing. I passed over the Useful Phrases part without a second glance. In languages where the same word has such hilariously different meanings, you could be saying just about anything. Better not even try. In a café in Laos, I'm told I once asked to be flogged. Now I just point. I took a quick gander at the tiny, useless map and proceeded to the local Don'ts. Don't, for instance, ever take a cyclo after dark, I was warned. Cyclos are the local three-wheel rickshaws with a little loveseat for two in front and a little guy sitting behind, pedaling and smiling homicidally. According to the guidebook, visitors who have taken cyclos after dark have been known to crawl home naked and bleeding. This item caught my faltering gaze because I had just seen a movie about the drivers of these nifty little craft and - call me romantic - I had already formed an image of them as a jolly band of brothers who would smilingly cut off your nuts for the price of a sandwich, a hard-working guild of picturesquely vicious little motherfuckers. I would *not* be taking a cyclo after dark.

I glanced up from my reading material and noticed that several of the beautiful submissives were now ritualistically binding themselves into jump seats. We were either approaching the climax of the floorshow, or Saigon.

We hit town at home-time on a late sunny afternoon. What a scene - a cascade of small people on wheels swirling around the city, eddying at red lights and swooshing off again like choreographed tsunamis at every green. It looked like one of those da Vinci studies in hydraulics. I swear I've met Australian surfers who could *ride* this shit. But it was all so toy and dainty and unthreatening, all flowing fabric and tinkling bells and bone-structure and poise. And the people themselves are all so unthreateningly un-large. I notice that I am a giant here. I positively *Gulliver* over these pretty wee folk. The fact that they are the pound-for-pound world champs of violence, pain, mayhem, torture and war - and would chew their own arms off to prove it - has not occurred to me yet.

Pretty soon I'm up in my room in the shiny new high-rise hotel I seem to have mistakenly booked myself into, sipping my courtesy Evian, wearing my courtesy slippers, picking my courtesy nose and staring out of the vacuum-sealed window at a view that's been sanitized for my protection. I'm trying to straighten out a bit from the recent river of booze by smoking a bit of the hashish I've just retrieved with great comic flair from my ass. Ah, yes. They can put a man on the moon, but there's still only one way to cross iffy borders while holding. And halfway down the joint I've just rolled, I'm already hating the joint I'm in. In crumbling old Saigon, this gleaming sky-scraper is about as real as three waltzing mice. From street level it looked like a very large marital aid left by very large, very horny aliens. From up here on the umpteenth floor, Saigon looks like that map in the guidebook, only smaller. It's like watching it all from the cheap seats. I'm way too high up here (and puff by magic puff getting way higher). It's all far too removed up here at the lubricated tip and it just feels too - dare one even whisper it? - too *safe?*

I decide to move, first thing tomorrow, to a real place, the kind of establishment where an international boulevardier such as I gets to shit in a hole in the floor. That's half the fun of being in the third world, isn't it?

It means you start the day with a sporting event even more forgiving than horseshoes. A near miss is not just OK. It's hilarious.

But first I have to get back down to the street and into all that swirling confetti. So I do. And that's where the trouble starts, because I'm highly impressionable at this point and a sucker for just about anything. And I've fallen in love with a dress. Not just any dress. *The* dress. The national dress. The *ao dai*. It's what all the local sweetie-pies were still wearing in those days. I was toast the moment I caught sight of my first ones as I was coming into town and the airport rivulet joined the main torrent. And by the flock and the flotilla, the passing *ao dais* had my head on a swivel. Somehow they contrived to make that Singapore Airlines fuck-me frock look like a wooden barrel.

The *ao dai* is the sartorial equivalent of the wolf-whistle. It is the most flattering garment ever devised for the female form and here every form was slim and dainty from nymphet to grandma. The *ao dai* hugs every tiny curve like paint, then falls to the floor in two long panels, one in the front, one at the back. As she climbs onto her bicycle, the delicate little figurine drapes the front panel over her slim wrist like a bridesmaid climbing a stair, exposing just a wink of nude torso above long pantaloons, a little sip of café au lait, and as she rides along, nipping in and out of the traffic, the back panel billows out behind her, tucked under her bite-size bottom, focusing all eyes on it, as a cupped hand does a flame. The *ao dai* has a high collar and it reaches all the way down to the tiny toes and yet, in the words of the ancient wag, 'It covers everything. It hides nothing.'

In satin, in silk, in mauve, in lavender, in icy blue and in dusky rose they glided up alongside you on quaint old sit-up bicycles with backs straight and pointy little breasts pointing the way home, black hair shiny and straw hats all at the perfect horizontal. Or they peeled out from you on their mopeds, negotiating the homicidal chaos like little seabirds diving for fishes, lunging and fading and whirling away. It looked as if all rehearsed simply to enchant and seduce. And it did.

So I just wanted to be back among all that. And once downstairs I almost ran out into the traffic, I was so humming with that feeling, those first few foolish moments in a place you've wanted to be in for a long time, when you're at street level and smelling it and you just can't believe you're actually there, the privilege of it all, all seemingly put on for your benefit alone. I just stood there amid the swirlage and the frockery, wondering what gauge of butterfly net I might need to snare one of these Eastern promises as they fluttered by in every pastel shade, keeping it all poetic at golden home time on this balmy Asian afternoon. And right there, through the flutter of fabric in the main square, I recognized another sigh-inducing sight - the old brown and cream colored Hotel Continental, where Graham Greene set his story of that jaded, faded Englishman and his uncatchable butterfly in her slinky *ao dai*, an airbrushed era ago. He cast a long shadow here at the end of the world, old Graham. Kids would run up to you, little angels with big eyes that looked right through you, and they all had the same three things to sell.

- You wanna postcards?

- No, thank you.

- OK, you wanna maps?

- No, thanks.

- OK, you wanna *the book?*

- The... book?

Yes. *The* book. Into your disbelieving hand is placed a paperback copy of *The Quiet American*. In Saigon apparently there was only one book. This was Nobel judgment incarnate right here in front of you in the shape of this eight-year-old, Eng Lit pusher, standing there with his little hand out. The Book has relegated the Vietnam War – or the American War as they call it here, more fairly - to a footnote. But Greene's war, the old war, the one against the French, is still doing boffo business. And who wouldn't rather read about guerrillas blowing up the colonial Frogs, and the Frogs all so fashionably dressed for it in their seersucker suits and their panama hats, with their noodle-thin Viet babes in their *ao dais* sailing among the mayhem, fabric aflutter, flitting like damsel-flies, unsullied, across this wild, whorish pond of the South, everywhere a little style, a little terror. They say history gets written by the winner. Not here. Here, for once, history has been written by the best writer.

I eye the girls longingly, sigh for them wistfully and weave my way unsteadily into a bar. It's a dark little joint and I have a vague connection with somebody who knows the manager. And here he is, sitting hunched on a barstool with his back to me, a long-haired ex-GI who wouldn't go home after the war. He's wearing a tee shirt on the back of which is printed in big letters *I Wasn't There And I Know Nothing*. A dark shade of Greene.

We talk. Outside, the darkening streets start to fill with tables. Sidewalk cafés materialize, filling the hot breeze with all manner of funky flaves. In no time at all I'm several scotches deeper in the bag and deeper still into conversation with shifty-looking ex-pats of every blood group, all of whom are speed-drinking and already several points shy of the vertical. I get many offers to be escorted to this dive and that, the better to explore what may lie, ahem, *beneath* the *ao dai,* so to speak. It seems that in this particular quarter, convenient to the ugliest of hotels and Americans, dear old Saigon is just one large whorehouse. I'm shocked, I say, shocked, and arrange to return later with a pocketful of local currency.

But first I have to eat and I don't want to eat here. Here it's all burgers and fries and I want something real and local, with at least a sporting chance of food poisoning. The owner tells me about this really good place that's 'not far', a spot that 'everybody knows' and that I 'can't miss'. So like a fool I leave. I stagger out into the street and the street is now fabulously transformed, awash with people and action. The sidewalks are covered with tables, the air full of the blue smoke and singed meat of various vermin and former pets, and in the gutters, between the parked cars, under the shade trees and anywhere they can find a space, there are now dozens of cyclos, their drivers lounging on their upholstered love-seats, smoking and talking amongst themselves. It's a movie. It's beautiful. It's seething. I'm ecstatic. I'm as stoned as a martyr.

More to the point, I've got the munchies. Now, where did he say that restaurant was? Where exactly was he pointing? It's all so dark and getting darker out there and a wee bit scary-looking, to tell the truth. I stumble over and ask the closest cyclo driver, a wrinkly old bird, for directions to the place. Yeah, sure, he knows it. It's not far. It's in that direction, over there, in the bleak, featureless, unlit, scary motherfucking dark. I stand there, following the direction of his bony claw pointing into the murky void. I can make out just one dark shape. It's lying in the middle of the road, way in the distance. It's me with my throat cut.

Behind me, the soothing voice of the old cyclo guy says softly, almost winsomely, "You like I take you there, boss? Not far. Only one dollar."

Ah, what do the guidebooks know, anyway, I say to myself as I sprawl sultan-like on the comfy little sofa of the old cyclo and we bounce off towards the restaurant. In a couple of blocks it's not even dark and scary any more. It's bright and colorful and insanely wonderful and I'm beside myself with joy. Now *this* is the way to travel. Just lay back and soak it in, hurtling through it all on a lunar divan, slumped like an addled pasha with a shit-eating grin. 'Oh, the places you'll go!' (And the state you'll be in).

And did I mention it was Friday night? Yes, flaming Friday night in steamy, sexy Saigon, the whole of downtown cranked up on raging hormonal gasoline, all dressed up and everywhere to go, everybody en route to clubs, bars and cafés, milling around and building up a head of steam for a big night on the town, everything out there over-cranked and over-amped, everywhere clusters of sharp little dudes with sharkskin suits and cigarettes, clumps of teeny little bad-girls giggling and smoking and pointing, open air clubs with bowel-moving sound systems revving up for later, making the wax run out of your ears and down your leg as you lurch by on your loveseat attached to a peddling maniac. The traffic is just one honking lava-flow, and this is not the purposeful, homeward-bound vortex of yester-hour. No siree, babe. This is a *parade*.

And now I'm not just looking at it from no stinkin' car. Now I'm in it. I *am* it, damn it. A cyclo is the ultimate vehicle in which to mingle and coalesce. Picture this. Wide avenues linked by big traffic circles, where nobody, but nobody, has the right of way, whatever those chicken-shit traffic lights may say. You may be large, you may be big-wheeled, multi-cylindered and full of flammable materials, but at every traffic circle and intersection, you have to give way to the biggest pair of balls. And the largest, swingingest *cojones* by far are jangling proudly between the legs of the cyclo drivers, all of whom have the same mission. They will get you, dead or alive, to where you're going, just slightly ahead of any other sonofabitch who dares get in your way. And they will do this not with speed, but with sperm-count. OK, the motorbikes, the cars, the trucks may overtake them on the straightaway. But come the roundabout and the crossroads, hold on, mama, this sumbitch is *coming through,* and they will gladly risk *your* life to make a point. Because you are their bumper! You're out there in front, feet first, in the middle of a demolition derby, on a *sofa.* And as they throw you at the oncoming traffic, playing chicken with *your* ass, their ultimate weapon is you. Because they know, or rather they gamble, that nobody in a car or a bus or a truck will be able to bring himself to actually *shear your frigging legs off.*

Plus, you have to understand that these people, like everybody else in Asia, practically *live* on two wheels. Pretty soon, Asian kids will roll out of the womb on two wheels to save time and cut out the middleman. "Feet? You got feet? How quaint." So within the traffic typhoon you're at sea on, there's all kinds of fancy riding and showing-off going on. And you are, remember, the beacon, the mark, the rube. Whatever may be your fancy-ass idea of yourself in the salons of Gay Paree, here you are a helpless schmuck. You are a chump, presented for all to see on the hurtling half-shell, on a bed of lettuce, on a plate, at the front of a low-speed chase on a goddamned *settee,* a magnet for attacks of weirdness from all sides. Not that this is a bad thing, you understand.

For instance, you're in the middle of traffic, flying but reclined. You're taking in the scene. You take out a cigarette. Suddenly on both sides of you there are two squealing dirt-bikes, veering in with a girl on the back of each one, two criminally pretty girls. And they're not wearing demure *ao dais* now baby, no sir. They're in ass-revealing micro-skirts with pert little posteriors poking out at you, and they're both reaching in with disposable lighters to light your cigarette, smiling fetchingly the whiles and saying demure little things like "Hey, you wanna follow me?

You wanna *fuck me? You wanna?"* Oh yes, girls. Yes, I do. And how thoughtful of you to ask. But, you see, I'm on my way to this *restaurant.*

There's no business like ho business. And there's no Chi Minh City like Ho Chi Minh City. It's all simply too fab. I mean, I've seen a few things, but a sultanic cyclocade with hooker outriders in stereo? I don't think so. And it went on and on like this. In the space of a few boulevards, I was offered, on the fly as it were, not just several portions of bite-size bootay, but an array of carnal services the gist of which I still cannot fully grasp to this day, even in the silence of my lonely room. But you get the picture. It was a whirligig, a blur of psychotropic fabulosity, and I didn't have enough too-easily-amused brain-cells available at this point to ask myself what I should, perhaps, have been asking myself for several miles now, which was: How long, exactly, have we been pedaling here, old sport?

What I first start to notice is not so much that my driver is now wheezing and grunting noticeably more than before, thereby marking a certain passage of time and effort. It's more the fact that all around me, the show is very gradually becoming less spectacular, then less interesting, then not interesting at all, then, well, *over.* The streets we are now in are still wide, but they're way less bustling. In fact, there's little or no bustle at all any more. Or people. Come to think of it. Now that you mention it. Coincidentally, all around me, it's getting incrementally darker.

Bit by little bit, like the slow sliding of a dimmer-switch, but happening so gradually that there's no real point at which you can say 'it's getting dark', it is getting dark. It's like a gradual blindness, except that in my case it's a gradual penny-drop. Yes, I do have to admit it, it is starting to get marginally murky around here and unmistakably un-central.

My dim bulb starts to form the airbrushed edge of a distant foggy thought. Could I be in the process of being - no it's too preposterous - but, could I be, foolish as it feels, in the throes of being, um, *kidnapped* by this bony, harmless-looking old fart behind me? Surely not. He could not be so ambitious. I turn around to look at him. He's dying of exhaustion, half my size and on the Jersey side of sixty. No, it's all too ridiculous. And yet...

Before I have time to weigh these ponderous thoughts, we come to a stop in the middle of nowhere on a dark and lonely avenue next to a beat-up old taxi. Leaning up against it are three guys, three thugs, three unmistakable jailbirds, just standing there grinning at me, looking me up and down, as if sizing up a cow on a meat-hook prior to chain-sawing.

One of them is a tough little bastard with a black bandana and filthy bare feet. His buddy has gold teeth and bow legs, and there's a third, equally fetching. They are all grinning at me. I am being positively beamed at by these three nasty pieces of work, while behind me my old pal is apparently expiring in a sputtering orgasm of phlegm. There is joy all around. I myself would smile, too, were I not so utterly f-f-fucking terrified.

Old cyclo-stiff to my rear gets a grip on his respiratory experience, and wheezes an explanation of this chilling turn of events. "I tired now, boss. Friends take you rest of way in taxi. Restaurant not far. Sorry, boss. OK?"

OK? Well, let's review the situation and see just how OK this is, shall we? I am stoned, drunk, lost and helpless. I'm in a dark and ugly corner of a strange and dangerous city. Not being familiar with a word of the local tongue, specifically the word *Help*, I am thus incapable of getting any, even if there were any and there isn't. I have a king's ransom of foldable American in my pants pocket. I am surrounded by a bunch of villains fairly licking their chops at the aroma of my wallet. If I run, they will catch me. If I hit them, they will stab me. Then they will rape, kill and eat me. If I simply give them my money, they will take it and may even say thank you. Then they will rape, kill and eat me. And as a first step towards doing all of the above, they want me to get into that filthy little shitbox, an alleged vehicle which probably doesn't even have an engine in it.

Slowly, with colossal effort, I drag my imminent corpse out of the cyclo and manage to stand fully erect. Once again I can't help noticing that I am over a foot taller than any of them. And once again I'm tickled pink by this utterly pointless point, considering that these are professional shanghai-artists, and I am the amateur half-wit who within two hours of landing in Saigon has waltzed his sorry ass into the radius of their bad breath. And anyway, I'm a coward. Ask anybody. I have only one hope, and it's a slim one. Maybe they will all just walk away in disgust when I soil myself.

I look at the taxi. I look longingly back down the dark avenue in the direction we have just come. I take one more look at the drooling cut-throats encircling me and see that I have two choices. I can either get in the car, or I can get in the car. I get in the car.

I sit there alone on the broiling back seat for a few seconds. For a few seconds it still seems possible that one of these decent, courteous taxi drivers might get behind the wheel, fire up this automotive husk and whisk me off to my dinner. It was still possible for around seven or eight seconds, as it turned out. At around seven or eight seconds and counting, all three muggers simultaneously climbed into the car and surrounded me, hemming me up against the rear door.

In the driver's seat in front of me, guy number three just sat there, staring through the windshield, smoking. He made no move whatsoever to start the car or even to pretend to. To his right was the coprophagic clown with the gold teeth, who turned around and flashed them at me even more fiercely than before. To my right, scary little bandana bastard squeezed right up against me. Outside my door, the scabrous old pedal pusher maneuvered his cyclo up against the rear door to obviate my putative egress, so to speak. I was fucked, so to speak.

The window of the door was missing and he looked in at me through the empty hole with a totally changed and truly fiendish expression, one of absolute triumph, as in *Gotcha*.

When it comes to fighting, the one thing I'm good at is getting beaten. My last public performance was typical of all the previous lowlights in my pugilistic career. I was working on a building site. It was a slapstick event, versus a big Irish lummox named Paddy, a fellow ditch-digger in that long summer of mud. We mauled each other around for a bit then flopped like drunken tango partners into a large puddle, to a sarcastic round of applause from our co-shoveling cohort standing around in a wet clump of boredom. By some piece of luck, I scrambled to my feet before he did and took a gorgeous swing at his vacant mug, as he lifted it up to me, gift-like. But at the last possible instant, the bastard raised up the handle of his big shovel to protect his chin and I broke two fingers on the thing and fell in a retching heap at his feet. Standing over me, he chivalrously handed me the lit cigarette he'd had in his mouth the whole time and I smoked it with as much aplomb as I could muster all the way to the emergency room.

Now this. Trapped in a car with three professional murderers. I had as much chance of getting out of this unscathed as a white suit has in a shit-fight.

I once saw Richard Pryor do this bit about why mugging Whitey is like taking candy from a baby. It's because Whitey lets you. It's true. We do. We would rather die at your mugging hands than suffer the indignity of turning on our heels and running or, God forbid, of actually *screaming at the top of our lungs for help*. He then showed us how he, as a dude of negritude, would react if *he* were mugged. He screamed. He ran around the stage in circles, bug-eyed, looking back over his shoulder, just screeching like a piglet. It was a riot. We all fell about. But it was a piece of generous advice from a brother. Don't just sit there, you dumb honky. *Scream and run, motherfucker. Scream and run.*

So, the moment Bandana Boy's hand shoots out and dives into my pants pocket, rooting around rudely and getting his filthy fingers around my cash, a fistful of *my* dollars, and it is finally obvious that there's no way in hell this is all going to turn out just ducky, I finally, *finally,* wake up and do my teacher proud. *I scream my dumb honky head off.*

Well, maybe scream is the wrong *verb*, Jack. What I was going for was a manly roar. But to judge by the horrified expressions on their faces, I gather that what came out sounded more like a donkey getting his nuts smashed between two bricks. God knows what the people on the street must have thought. "There's a donkey in there getting castrated? In that little car with no engine in it? How the hell did they persuade the stupid fucker to get *in?*"

So I'm just braying my head off. And that opens the floodgates. Decades of ingrained Whiteytude exit my pie-hole on the roaring tide. And while I'm honking away for dear life, I haul back and crack the guy as hard as I can with my elbow, right in the kisser. *Bam!* I'm more surprised than he is. Oh, that *had* to hurt. And it occurs to me that I've always wanted to do that. So I do it again. *Bang!* Right on the snout. There's claret pumping all over the show. The guy's moaning and holding his bleeding schnozz and the gilded muppet in the passenger seat is just frozen, because you have to understand that in the middle of all this hitting and hemorrhaging, *I'm still braying like a donkey!*

Nobody has moved, nobody but me. So I feel rather encouraged. I squeeze my legs out of the tiny space I'm crammed into and kick the passenger-seat guy right in the face with my foot. It's a sickening blow. He slumps back against the window. Wow. This is great. I've never kicked anybody before in my entire life. I've never even seen a Jackie Chan movie. I'm a softy, a milquetoast. Ask anybody. I have no *idea* where all this is coming from, this mini-fit of John Waynery. It must be from some never-wakened brainstem ganglia that governs the fear of Dying Like A Total White Tit.

I start pushing at the door with my shoulder, but there's no give. So I wriggle and squirm and squeeze my body through the little window, thanking God I'm a scrawny twerp and push off against the bleeding guy next to me, one last goodbye foot in the head to get me all the way out. I roll headfirst in slow motion onto the pavement, oozing somehow between car and cyclo like a long vehicular bowel movement onto the road. And get this - *I'm still hollering like a deranged pack-animal!*

I'm just roaring my head off as I scramble to my feet, my nice white shirt hanging off me in shreds due to the scraping exit, and copiously decorated with the other guy's blood. I can't believe I'm out. I can't believe I just did what I did. Even more, I can't believe that, even now, nobody has moved, nobody but me. Not even old death-rattle over here, staring at me in total Asiatic disbelief.

We're eye to eye, him and me, face to face. He's perched up there on his spindly old apparatus, giving me the same look of horror your maiden aunt might if you threw all your toys out of your cot. So I squat down and grab one large cyclo wheel in both hands, and with surprisingly little effort, like lifting a big bamboo bird-cage, I slowly stand up with it. The delicate contraption pitches slowly over, taking the old villain with it and depositing him gently onto the macadam before crashing rather daintily on top of him with a plaintive little *pling pling.*

I look around at the street. Oh, shit. *Everybody* is looking. Cars have stopped. Women have their hands up to their mouths in horror, no kidding. Not, I guarantee you, because somebody is getting robbed, raped, killed and eaten. I'm sure that's par for the course in this neighborhood. No, it's the surreal vision of a blood-covered white man standing in the middle of an Oriental thoroughfare, yodeling his head off like some inbred hog-farmer calling the pigs in.

So I shut up. I just turn and leg it out of there as fast as I can run, my shredded, blood-stained shirt flapping behind me like an *ao dai* on a rodeo clown, as my fifteen seconds of winning is up, and it suddenly occurs me that I'm now in much deeper shit than before. I'm still drunk, stoned, lost and helpless. But now, any second, those three junkyard dogs are going to come out of shock and come after me, and now they have a righteous *reason* to kill me.

I run right down the middle of the avenue. Every few steps I look back over my shoulder, like Richard Pryor, to see if the dogs are on me yet. They're not. I make it around the corner un-pursued. Now I'm half jogging, half walking. Not because it will attract any less attention, given my appearance, but it feels a tad less unseemly, somehow, my whiteytude seeping back at an alarming rate.

It's brighter here and busier. And suddenly, there in front of me - Buddha be praised - is a taxi, an escape module, a cute little cab of the regular, non-mugging fleet, sitting at the curb with an angelic old geezer behind the wheel reading his newspaper. It's *Deliverance.* Just like the movie. But without Burt Reynolds and the rubber suit. Minutes later I'm out of there. I'm saved. I'm in one piece and my money is still in my pocket. It's all over. I'm slumped in the back of the cab, calming down, motoring back towards the center of town to my suddenly-beloved hotel with its safety-chain, its digital key and its pomaded musclemen in the lobby. Each avenue we turn into becomes progressively brighter and more full of Friday nightly color and crowds. I start to recognize landmarks. I'm on the right track. I'm rescued. I'm going home. I sink into the comfort of the plastic backseat, cadging a cig from Nguyen, my driver and new best friend, blowing plumes of dove-grey smoke into the navy-blue night. Ah yes. This is the life, eh? Visit foreign lands. Meet exotic people. Kick their teeth in.

A few blocks more and I'm already doing all the social arithmetic, converting what had befallen me from horror into currency, a tale to tell, something to dine out on, a real adventure, an escape, a close one, touch and go, something for the lads to laugh at, definitely worth a few free drinks, and even more potent of course, for the girls. Pure gold. Chateau Leg-Opener 1978. "Um, well, to be perfectly honest, my sweet, I admit I was momentarily fazed, but I'm rather adept at a specialized form of in-cab karate, you see, and I believe I did already mention that I positively *Gullivered* over these people..."

- Why you go there?

Little Nguyen rouses me from my mental tongue-bath.

- Excuse me?

- Why you go there?

- Why I go where?

- Why you go Chinatown?

- Chinatown?

- Why you go Chinatown? Chinatown number one bad.

- Ah. Chinatown.

- Number one bad.

- That was Chinatown. Yes. I knew that.

- Why you go? You stupid?

- No. I was, er... visiting friends.

- You get rob?

- No. Just visiting friends.

- Why you cover in blood? You get rob.

- No. I love Chinatown, actually.

- You stupid.

- Is there any music in this cab?

My droll chauffeur and I continued our lively chat in this informative vein for a few more blocks as I learned all the terrifying details of the foul quarter I had just been sprung from. Chinatown, eh? Number one bad. Well, well. Of course, this new and even scarier revelation made absolutely no impression on my ungrateful soul, as far as thanking Buddha for my undeserved salvation. No, I was already far too busy refining the leg-over routine, back in the old US of A-cup.

"And of course, my pet, this all went down in darkest Chinatown, you understand. Hellhole of the Orient, don't ya know. Oh, yes. Once, at the mere mention of Saigon Chinatown, Jackie Chan is said to have soiled himself. Another splash of Chateau Bendover, my little pomegranate?"

Ungrateful cur that I am, I do not once, not for a second and not until months later in the total recall of my sweat-soaked middle-of-the-night shivering bed, not once do I even whisper to myself how lucky I am and what a prick. No, right now I am aglow. I had actually hit people. *Me!* I had not gone gently. Nah, not me. No, siree. I had walked out onto that *High Noon* street and faced down those bad boys, just like Gary Cooper, but without the big hat. And as I gaze out of the cab window into the passing neon blur, the movie credits start to roll and here's Grace Kelly looking up at me, face awash in tears of admiration and naked lust, and we start to hear the first notes of that famous theme-tune, "Do not forsake me, oh my darlin' ... oh, my... *OH MY GOD!!!!*

BAM! A fist hits the window right next to my day-dreaming face. *BOP!* A foot hits the window opposite. It's them! Oh sweet taxi-driving Jesus! It's *all of them*, all four horsemen on two yowling dirt-bikes, one on each side, two thugs per, kicking the cab and punching it. They're barking, raving mad, eyes bulging with venom and they're all screaming at poor little Nguyen to stop. He doesn't know what to do. He's looking around in horror. He probably knows all their prison records by heart. He looks around at me in abject terror and starts gabbling at me and pleading with his attackers. His cab is skewing all over the road, and he's - oh God no - he's slowing down. *Oh, Noooo!!!!*

"No!!! Don't slow down, I'm begging you, man. I'll give you money, mucho mucho dollars. Look, man. Mucho dollars!" (yes, I do appear to be speaking in Spanish at this point, and no I don't know why, OK?) I lean over the front seat and show him enough flapping greenery to *buy* the frigging cab outright, but he's - oh no - he's slowing down even more. And the maniacs have started leaning in off their dirt bikes like rodeo cowboys, trying to rip open the doors. I jump forward and knock down both the door-locks, thanking Buddha that they work. "Oh man," I keep mumbling aloud to nobody, "oh man, oh man, oh man, I'm in deep shit now. I'm in deep, deep, deep shit now."

And now they go to work on Nguyen full-throttle, from both sides, waving their fists and speed-gabbling at him on both channels. They're pounding on the roof and, weirdest detail of all, the old cyclo driver, who's riding on the back of the right-hand bike is just staring at me, just leering unblinkingly.

It's like he's trying to scare me, or something. Why? Does he not know that *actual shit* is actually threatening to run down my *actual leg* at this *actual moment?*

They're all over the cab now, practically hugging it. We're going slower and slower. I'm holding poor little Nguyen, shaking his shoulders and waving my money and begging and whining and in between just wailing over and over at nobody, "Oh man, oh man, oh man, I'm in deep, deep, deep shit now."

And we're slowing. We're slowing. We're going slowly enough now that pedestrians are starting to notice the passing fracas and trucks and cars behind us are honking. And old cyclo guy is just staring at me ghoulishly, like a very *un*-enlightened Buddha, licking his bony lips in anticipation of… of… of what I daren't even imagine. And then, just as we begin to crawl so slowly that they could all jump off those bikes and climb onto the cab, and just as I'm about to pass out from pure fright, something happens, something totally unexpected.

Far away in some forgotten corner of Heaven, an unemployed guardian angel turns away from his TV program and raises one eyebrow. A molecule moves and the universe realigns.

Cyclo guy, subtly but unmistakably, makes the international signage for money. You know the one. He rubs his grimy thumb and middle finger together. And with that one tiny little finger-thumb rub-a-dub, the brown cloud of terror lifts. Suddenly I'm in territory I understand. I can deal. I'm still in shit, but this is shit I can swim in. I open the right-hand window just a crack and yell at him "OK. How much you want, motherfucker?" And you know what he says? "Ten dallah!" I can't believe my ears. I have to ask again. He repeats the amount, with a curled lip, as if to say "You heard me right, asshole, ten *large*." Ten dollars? *Ten?* Is that what this is all about? The difference between life and castration is the price of an egg-salad sandwich and a large coffee?

I lean back against the pink plastic and peel off a ten. But then - I don't know why, it's so nuts, but somehow it feels like the right thing to do - I put the money down and yell out of the cracked-open window "No! Fuck you! I hold up the splayed fingers of one hand. "I give you five, motherfucker! *Five!*" And a smile of sweet victory lights up his face and he actually looks almost adorable for a moment, in a toothless, halitosis sort of way. He shouts something to his driver, his driver yells at the other two guys on the other side of the cab and, all together they start yelling, but happily, gleefully "Fy dallah! Fy dallah! Fy dallah!" And with my most magnanimous, southern-diplomat, baby-kissing smile and in my bloodstained tatters, I roll down the window all the way and grandly hand over five U.S. like a visiting bigwig handing out some kind of diploma for first-class highway-robbery. 'Jolly good. Well done. Well mugged. Carry on.' And there is joy, pure mercantile joy in Mudville, brethren and sistren, joy all around.

They pump their fists in the air. They whistle and they whoop. And then they all peel out and disappear into the traffic, yelling "Mathafacka! mathafacka! mathafacka!' just to piss me off. And that is that. They are gone.

Five bucks. Well, I'll be dipped in shit. I slump back onto the backseat and start thinking politically correct thoughts, despite myself. I think about how livid it used to make me, when I was young and livid and slightly to the left of The Baader-Meinhof Gang, this gulf between rich nations and poor. Nothing's changed. It is still the wretched of the earth who make it possible for the price of my freedom to be so comically small and for the third world to be my oyster. But I'm no longer young, no longer livid, no longer quite so good, I guess. So fuck them and their five bucks. As my Great Aunt Sarah used to say so poetically, I hope they get boils on their ass.

Back at the hotel, climbing out of my salvation wagon, I tip my trusty driver a week's wages, which he'll need for the opium he'll have to smoke for his blood pressure. But old Nguyen, even more than the money, clearly values the good line, the parting shot, our common weakness, international ironists that we both are. And sure enough, with minimal English, the old boy gets it off, the last word.

- Nice friends.
- Excuse me?
- Nice friends you have. In Chinatown.
- Ah.
- Number one nice.

SAME SAME

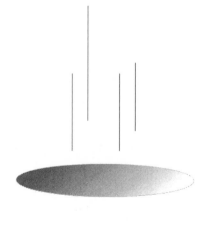

BANGKOK

'To Asian girls, all white men look alike.'

I had heard this goofy piece of local knowledge many times from otherwise-sane-looking Western men all over Asia. The observation was always delivered with a straight face, but it always cracked me up. I never took it seriously. So it never really sank in. It never occurred to me that it might conceivably be true, until one night in Bangkok.

It was one of those hot, steamy monsoon nights, with warm puddles reflecting the neon and the streetlights, all very exotic and *noir* and just like in the movies. I was lying on a big bed in a small hotel, flat on my back, head on a pillow. The room was on a high floor overlooking a warren of little backstreets in the Nana district. The word *nana,* by hilarious coincidence, also happens to be the French slang for the kind of girl you would be most likely to *meet* on a hot and steamy Bangkok backstreet at night. So the district of Nana is well named, in a French sort of way, if you catch my drift.

At the other end of the bed, kneeling between my splayed legs, was the lovely little Yaya. Yaya was a Nana *nana*. She was at that moment giving me a foot massage. And she was humming a sweet little tune in her sweet little voice, while gazing absently out of the open window. It was a lovely languid moment, she humming, I drifting. Listening to her tiny voice reminded me of how as a little boy I had always loved to tinkle the highest keys on the piano. She stopped humming as a thought came to her.

- You same same another guy.

- Excuse me?

- You. Another guy. Same same.

- You know someone just like me?

- Same same.

- Shouldn't you be saying there's nobody quite like me?

- This guy same.

- Oh.

Humming. Drifting. Humming. Drifting.

- Like me in what way?

- Oh, you know. Same face. Same thin. Same tall. Same make joke.

- Ah. He likes to make you laugh, too?

- Joke, joke, joke. Same, same, same. Same this.

She pointed to my glasses

- So you mean this guy is exactly like me in every way?

- Same other guy, same you.

- Well, in that case he sounds… *fantastic!*

- Oh, come on, Yaya, I should meet this character. It could be fun, Let's give him a call. We should all have a drink together. It would be a laugh, don't you think? You have his number?

- Have.

- Great. Call him.

- Can not.

- Why not?

- He go away.
- Oh. Pity. How long ago?
- Six month ago? One year ago? I don't remember.
- Oh well.
- He stay in big hotel. Ambassador Hotel.
- The Ambassador?
- He take my photo, too. Very nice photo. You like look my photo?
- Sure. I'd love to. Let's take look at this other guy's shot of you.
- OK.

So she leaned over and rummaged around in her big red bag lying open on the corner of the big bed. She pulled out a Polaroid and handed it to me and then went back to massaging my feet, so gently, humming her sweet little lullaby in her sweet little voice.

I pushed my glasses to the end of my nose and looked at the picture. Yes, it really was a *very* good shot of her. I had to admit he had captured exactly what made Yaya so adorable, standing there with her head tilted fetchingly to one side, just so, trying to look coy in that pornographically short dress, in front of those tall red Ambassador curtains.

Yes. A lovely shot. I remembered taking it.

SHIT BOMB

TOKYO

The Language Barrier is generally held to be a bottomless pit of potential embarrassment for the traveler. But that view does not take into account the traveling pervert.

There are those among us who simply *cannot* be embarrassed. We have no shame, no pride. We are the clowns, the hams, the guys who truly do *not* give a fuck, who will do just about anything for a laugh, and if those laughs are directed at ourselves? Well, what's your point, exactly?

We are the stage-hogs, the ones who actually *court* the opportunity to make total tits of ourselves in public. For us, the language barrier is not so much a barrier as a bar, a bar that is always being raised. We raise it ourselves, because to us it's a sporting event, and a competitive one at that, with degrees of difficulty and style points and awards, just like in the Olympics. For us, any attempted communication that ends up with an entire village pointing at us and laughing hysterically is equivalent to a perfect 10 triple back-flip. With pike. It's a drug.

And it's an addiction that creeps up on you by degrees. You're not born with it. But once hooked, you're toast. Once addicted, and having had to Charlie Chaplin your way through enough bizarre situations in strange places, you start to believe that you can get your meaning across, eventually, to absolutely *anybody*. At this point, your traveling life becomes a silent movie with a laugh track.

You start to actually look around for challenges. It's quite possible that some of the people who disappear annually into the jungles of Borneo, never to re-emerge, are just junkie arm-wavers like me who went in there just to see if they could pull off the feat of ordering, from a headhunter, an *actual head* 'with the tahini sauce, but without the onions.'

I should mention that I am pretty world-class at this event. I can gesticulate my ass off to great effect. And I too believed I could get over any *thing* to any *body* right up to the moment when I had to explain to a roomful of very proper Japanese matrons that I had not had a bowel movement for two weeks and that if I didn't get something to un-bung my bung-hole, and pronto, there was such a Mount Fuji of backed-up *umgawa* in there that I might explode at any second and redecorate their little teahouse in autumnal shades of flung dung. But more of that presently.

That level of challenge is found only at the extreme end of the sport, to be attempted only by professionals. This is because failure can make the amateur gun-shy and stunt his growth in The Craft. He must be reassured constantly that even an old pro like myself can crash and burn on the simple, bunny-slope stuff. It *will* happen. The failures *will* come. One has to simply shake them off, stay focused, stay in training, take it one day at a time and remember it can happen to the best.

For example, one night in Cambodia I was in a taxi, driving into Phnom Penh from the countryside and I was bursting for a pee, nearly wetting myself. As my Italian friend would say, my back teeth were *bathing*. Every few hundred yards, knowing not a single word of Khmer, I agitatedly pointed to my crotch and begged the driver to stop. Simple stuff. Piece of cake, normally. But he just kept waving me away, saying, "Here no good. Here no good." I couldn't understand why he was being so prudish.

I was practically squirting, and it was pitch black out there. Nobody would have seen me relieving myself by the roadside, nor would they have given a rat's ass. This was, after all, *Cambodia*, for Christ's sake - hardly a vortex of propriety. We had just driven through an entire Village of Whores, for crying out loud, a whole zip code of criminally underage coochy standing there in the middle of the street practically *brandishing* their vaginas at us.

And that place is the target of more enthusiastic tourism than all of the frigging temples combined. So what the hell was his problem here? But the more I kept pointing desperately to my lap and putting my palms together in the international sign of supplication, the more he kept waving me off and plowing into the night at a fiendish pace. I was on the point of Super-Soaking his vinyl when he finally screeched to a halt by a road-side shop, ran in, ran out, jumped back in the cab and, with a look of total toothy triumph handed me a large pack of condoms.

Whu..? What could he *possibly* have been thinking? That I found him so attractive I simply had to have safe sex with his hairy little ass that very *minute?* But my bladder was stretched so squeaky tight by this point that it felt like one of those yard-long balloons that clowns twist into sausage dogs, so I couldn't care less if he was raving or just retarded. I had to *go,* baby. So I thanked him politely for the rubbers, opened my door, climbed out of the cab very gingerly, afraid of, so to speak, 'going off' accidentally, walked very carefully around to the front of his taxi, stood there in his high-beams, the better to clarify the situation for him, unzipped my pants and *power-hosed* the dried mud off his front bumper and didn't stop until all four tires were cooling off in a small lake. As the penny finally dropped, all he said was "Ah!" It was possibly the only sound our two languages had in common.

But he was a sport, I must say. The rest of the way back into town, he kept looking over at me and slapping his own forehead - the international signage for 'I'm a moron' - and smiling to himself. I knew exactly what was going through his mind. "What was I thinking? That he had to have safe sex with my hairy little ass that very minute?"

You, however, are unlikely to have the luxury of such a simple demo. Generally speaking, you will have to act the whole thing out, *whatever it is*, and that's where the years of practice pay off for those among us who actually live for the so-called 'awkward sitch', because for us there is no such thing. For us there is only glory, there is only the gold.

One classic of the repertoire that comes to mind is the comic challenge of having to communicate, *in mime,* that your girlfriend needs a tampon. Picture that for a moment. Ask yourself. How would *I* act that one out? That's one I really look forward to. For a crack that particular Everest, I have been known to volunteer on behalf of total strangers. Hey, you'll never see these people again. What do you care? Give 'em a command performance, I say. Go for the jugular. Leave 'em laughing. Give 'em an encore. Use props! Oh, you may not get your tampon, but you might get a round of applause, or a free drink, and an Oscar nod is a distinct possibility.

In my own case, I believe it was that Tokyo shit-bomb scenario I was just mentioning that brought me the closest to being tapped for the old statuette. It all began with a shouted conversation with a Japanese guy in a very loud nightclub in New York City.

- Aran!
- Yes?!
- Aran, you funny guy!
- Yes?!
- You are!
- I am?
- We all raff at you!
- You do?!
- We raff at you a *rot!*
- Really?
- We *urinate!*
- Thank you very much!
- We want to make you an offer! We want you to be our deejay! In Tokyo! At our big convention!
- I'll do it!

- But before you say yes or no, Aran-San, you should know that we have hired many very beautiful girls to work with you!
- I'll do it!
- We have booked some of the most beautiful models in all of Japan! And you would be their boss, Aran! They would all be working for *you!* Get picture?!
- Got picture! I'll do it!
- However, money not good! Only $3,000!
- Only $3,000?!
- Yes!
- I'll *pay it!*
- Oh, ha ha ha! See! You very funny guy!
- That's a very old joke, Katsu!
- So you accept?!

Accept? I would have done it for food. So, a couple of weeks later I'm stretched out, drunk and disorderly, across an emperor-sized bed on a high floor of a very flash hotel in the very flash Ginza district of Tokyo, my lifeless body an empty canvas for swirling, pulsating colors bouncing off the world's most expensive neon, dancing up and down the buildings around me and reflecting off my drunken ass, lighting me up like a jukebox through my floor-to-ceiling wall of glass. I am spread-eagle on satin, bleary-eyed and gawking at the whole silly shebang, exhausted from the polar night flight and deep in the bag from the river of hot sake that followed our flight-path.

Lying there half dead but fully delighted, I have to smile at the very thought that I might have said no to *this* gig. For a start, the measly 3 Gs they paid me was exactly $3,000 more than I had in the world at the time. They had no way of knowing that, of course. Or *did* they, those subtle bastards? Did I give off the deadly 'broke' aroma, I wonder? Did they intuit my straits from my aura? Is that what they were all yapping about prior to the formal offer? "Listen guys, this fucker's penniless, I can *smell* it. Let's offer him 3 Gs and keep the other 7 Gs for hookers!"

Was that it? Oh, who cares? Spread it around, I say. Like the guy said in *Lawrence of Arabia*, I am a river to my people.

All that mattered to me was that I was here on my first visit to the land of the rising prices and if I hadn't been feeling like hammered dogshit, I would have been dancing on the ceiling along with the colored lights. How I swung this job I could barely believe. There was this little bunch of Japanese advertising guys visiting New York and I showed them around a bit, that's all. And they never let me spend a cent during the entire good time. Plus, I personally drank most of their per diems, all lavished on top-shelf liquor. But somehow they still felt that they owed me a debt of gratitude - an impression I did nothing to dispel - and they assured me that they would make it all up to me in Tokyo.

And they really did. In exchange for what they considered the paucity of the foldable, they finessed something far more attractive to my way of thinking. A tab. They had organized for me a rolling, floating, cumulative, generalized, open-ended, open-*sandwich* sort of expense account that was pretty much good for anything Within Reason, quote unquote. I resolved to find out, a.s.a.p. where the outer perimeter of Reason might be located, exactly.

So, prone and bushed tho I was, I was also in the process of truffling through the long list of hotel services enshrined in the bible-size leather tome spread out in front of me on the bed, when my bloodshot eye stumbled across the one item that fairly *snorted* to be the first test of my new best friend, the tab. I picked up the phone.

- Hello?
- Good evening, sir.
- I see that you offer massage.
- Yes, sir.
- Can I have one in my room?
- Yes, sir. Man or woman, sir?
- Woman. Er... small woman.
- I beg your pardon, sir?
- Petite.

- She *is* a very skilled masseuse, sir.
- Yes, but is she petite?
- Sir?
- And is she young?
- Why do you ask, sir?
- And pretty?
- Sir, your questions…
- Yes?
- Small, Young. Pretty...
- Yes?
- This is not that kind of massage, sir.
- What kind?
- You know, sir. *That* kind.
- Oh. I see. Well. Um. Of course not. I don't *want* that kind.
- No, sir. Of course not.
- But, just as a matter of interest...
- Yes, sir?
- Is she big?
- No, sir.
- Is she old?
- No, sir
- Is she ugly?
- No. sir.
- Can I charge her to my room?
- Yes, sir.
- Send her up.

Galvanized into action, I positively *dervished* around the room, clearing the bed of the usual detritus - the hashish smuggled in up my startled rectum and retrieved with the usual comic flourish a short time earlier and already half smoked; my one literary purchase at the airport, *Tokyo Schoolgirls In Uniform*, and the umpteen drained bottles of mini-bar liquor of every hue and flave. I smoothed the bed and lurched into the bathroom to attempt a quick ablute in prep for the old magic fingers

37

and who knew what else.

The bathroom of this particular designer boutique hotel had been ventured in the Gay Samurai motif. It was dominated by a chest-high wooden bathtub that was actually a huge wooden barrel sitting on its end and full of hot water, just like in *Throne Of Blood*, but without the disemboweling. There was a daintily distressed wooden stool and wooden pail and a big drain in the middle of the floor. It was intended to look rustically butch for the hard-charging A-type business stud, I imagine, but – to be brutally frank - it might have appealed more to a transvestite shepherdess.

I yanked open the barrel lid and stuck my elbow in to test the waters. Mmmmm. Like hot sake. I climbed in and sank down onto the little wooden shelf with a whimper of ball-coddling joy, knees pulled up, chin on knees and water over my chin, in hot, wet heaven. I felt like a drunken fetus. I was just about to let go a languid fart of unborn bliss, when Whoops! I suddenly remembered. You're not supposed to do this, are you? You're supposed to wash yourself first, *before* you get in so you can soak in clean water, instead of in your own barbaric Western filth. I remembered, once again, that the Japanese word for foreigner - *gaijin* - if written in a certain way is… unflattering.

So I heaved the sleepy gaijin - unflattering version - out of the big tub and squatted it on the tiny stool. I proceeded to soap it and scrub it, filling the little wooden pail with clean water from the tap and pouring it over myself repeatedly until I was squeaky clean and watching the whole sudsy jizz disappear down the drain in the middle of the floor. I climbed back into the warm wooden womb, feeling as if I had returned to heaven, but this time as a saint.

I re-positioned the gleaming scrotum onto the shelf and placed the gleaming chin on the gleaming knees and this time I let out a long and elaborate submarine fart of such melodious sonority that it sounded like a humpback whale trying out as a lounge singer.

- Hello sir.
- Whu…

- Ready, sir?
- Whu…
- Your massage, sir.
- *Whu?*

I opened my eyes to an apparition. Had I died and ascended? In front of me was an angel holding open a fluffy white robe, her arms spread wide like a little girl describing how big something is, a plumpish little angel with dimples and a halo, surrounded by twittering little bluebirds. She was a maternal sort of angel in a nurse's outfit, or maybe an angel's mom who also worked as a nurse part-time, I couldn't decide which. The hot water had knocked me sideways. I had fallen asleep instantly, chin on knees. I felt like a goofy Marat, stabbed with a rubber chicken.

The Herculean labor of willing myself out of the water and into the beckoning bathrobe was like Sisyphus pushing a big lump of flubber up a hill of molasses. I leaned on the poor little masseuse all the way to the big bed and then just basically fell on it and her. But she was a trooper. She got onto the bed with me and was all business, sitting back on her bare heels, rolling my dead weight this way and that to get me out of the robe and onto a towel, clucking and prattling away at me as she kneaded my corpse into a boneless puddle that could be poured into any vessel. I watched her through lowering, heavy lids as her dimpled fingers moved over me, and crazy neon colors splashed like tutti frutti ice cream up and down her crisp white uniform and over my soft pink body. The curtain came down slowly, very slowly, on this psychedelic and oddly sexy little nocturne, my last thought before fade-out being to picture *this* little woman giving me *that* kind of massage. Maybe later. Something to sleep on, eh?

Yes, sir.

But I don't want *that* kind of massage, you understand.

No, sir. Of course not, sir. Goodnight, sir.

Next morning, bright and bushy, the ad boys seemed very pleased to see me at their big shiny agency, welcoming me to Japan, having me sit in on a 'creative conference' at which tall glasses of very good scotch were demolished and refilled and everyone referred to me, to my face, as 'the gaijin' and I just *knew* it was the unflattering spelling. But I was so impressed by the fact that they all drank scotch like tea, at noon, served by cute young girls who *bowed,* for god's sake, that I was not at all put out. Do ad guys still do that, I wonder? But anyway all was forgiven when they led the gaijin, with much nudging and tittering, to the main event.

At the end of a long, oak-paneled corridor, a big double-door was heaved aside and I was waved into a grand room that was almost filled by a vast round table, an expanse of mahogany big enough for the entire national assembly to surrender to somebody at. The boss waved me to the front, to see what they were all giggling at and nudging each other over. I could barely believe it when I saw it.

In a circle all the way around the table were thirteen - count 'em - thirteen heavenly young creatures, the promised models, the promised land. They were the most electrifying thirteen of anything I had ever seen placed next to each other, thirteen babes, a wanker's dozen, with tiny hands folded demurely in tiny laps, all sitting up very straight, facing front and fairly bristling with perk, all staring at me, ("Remember, Aran San, you will be their boss. Get picture?")

Got picture. The boss said something to them and they all smiled politely, in unison. And then they all slowly - get this - they all slowly bowed. To *me.* In *unison.* And they kept their pretty little noses almost touching the table for an erotic eternity, in unison. Then they all sat upright again and stared at me, in unison, this time all giggling girlishly. God's holy trousers. I nearly began pogo-dancing and barking like a seal. In unison.

The entire rest of my life went by in a bit of a blur after that, it's high point. But I shall try to recall a few details.

After work, the boss took us out on the first of what would become a series of spectacular dinners, the first one held in a joint so fancy we each had our own geisha, in full drag, kneeling beside us, hand-feeding us with chopsticks, tittering respectfully at every bon mot and getting us legless by refilling all our glasses after every single sip. When I was drunk enough, I did my 'stoned samurai' impersonation to such acclaim that the boss dragged us all to his private club as a reward. It was a very swank affair indeed.

A door was opened on a whispered password and we sank into a cream colored carpet that came over our socks. I looked around. A Venetian glass chandelier of Phantom-of-the-Op dimensions illuminated what at first seemed like a dark, high-ceilinged library full of plush leather couches and walls of books, until one's eyes adjusted and the books revealed themselves to be hundreds of bottles of single malt, each one with a medallion bearing the name of its owner. Center stage, beneath the chandelier, was a full-size black Steinway concert grand with a full-on geisha on the stool in a psychedelically scarlet kimono head slightly bowed, hands in lap, awaiting instruction. We were ushered by other geishas to our buttery leather booth and the boss's eighteen-year Macallan was retrieved with great hoo-ha from its high shelf by yet another geisha in the full Kurosawa, on one of those high library ladders on wheels. I had entered a rarified realm.

In the half-gloom all around, tinkling geisha giggles harmonized with the clinking of cut crystal as deals were done, reputations ruined and blame assigned. We drank and we talked, though the gaijin was somewhat removed from the general conversation, busy looking around at the details of this inner sanctum. From time to time, members or guests would rise from their dimpled leather and approach a rococo lectern adjacent to the Steinway. There they would flip through a studded tome, would find something to their liking, would say something to the piano figurine, who would then begin to accompany them politely in their chosen song. This was karaoke of such a refined ilk it was barely recognizable to civilians. This was the Karnegie Hall of Karaoke.

And it was clearly not meant as frivolity but as a bonding mechanism among the highest of echelons, an exercise in the semiotics of seniority, a handing down of the key to the executive bathroom from cufflink to button, as bespoke bosses invited off-the-peg subordinates to perform for the general amusement, which they all did of course, instantly, tone-deaf and tuneful alike, choosing a song, nodding to the geisha and baritoning it politely. Every rendition was greeted with the same blank round of polite applause. Nobody really paid any attention. It was a social thing, a guy thing, a corporate thing. You were asked to sing. You sang. You were OK. I was fascinated. I was mesmerized. I was also, by this time, ripped to the tits on the finest single-malt that had ever whetted my Western whistle. And the whiskeyer I got, the more appalled I became by the musical stylings of these suburban suits. That was a big fat book they had to choose from over there, and yet they all seemed to go for the same song. *Autumn Leaves*. In Eng-rish. "Those farring *reaves* / da-lift by my window / those autumn *reaves* / of led and gold…" To the gaijin this was an outrage. All that material to choose from and they all trotted out the same tune? Hey, it's a nice wee ditty, chaps, but enough already. The shit-face gaijin clearly had a lot to learn about consensus, about not sticking out, about not making waves. He had yet to learn about *everything that really matters* here in the land of the rising - but not rising too far above the rest - sun.

As if on culture-cue I felt a dig in my ribs and my wandering attention was politely redirected to my host, the boss. He was gesturing to me to perform. It was my turn. Well, hey now. I could not refuse, would not have *dreamt* of refusing, this far into the bag. I got up and bowed to him deeply. Then I strode very unsteadily towards the lectern and flipped through the fat hymnal.

I actually laughed out loud as I read through the long list of incredible stuff that was available for performance, not believing that it really was. Sweet lip-synching Jesus. I looked over towards the geisha at the grand. She was smiling back at me. I asked her, incredulously, "Number 102?" She said, "Yes. OK." I was in shock. I asked her again and got the same reply. There could be no mistake. She could actually *play* number 102? Or at least she was willing to *have a go?* It seemed impossible. But all my guys were now staring at me and gesturing encouragement. So I just nodded to the little woman and said, "OK, then. Number 102… *hit it!*"

Until this soon-to-be-famous moment, I gather that this particular venue had never before been exposed to the *oeuvre* of Little Richard.

The response was *electrifying*. Everybody in the joint sat bolt upright, as if their collective cock had been jammed into the collective wall socket. They all yanked their heads around to stare as the little woman hammered down on the keys with her two little fists like a deranged doll, and I put my head back and let rip with "Tutti fruttti / Ah rooty / Tutti frutti / ah rooty / Tutti friuti / Ah rooty / Tutti friuti / Ah rooty / Tutti friuti / Ah rooty / A wham bama loomah / A lam bam boom!..."

And we were *off!* She banged away and I just wailed through every goofy verse, both of us egging each other on and grinning like idiots. It was hilarious. We were great. We *killed*. At the final flourish, she jumped to her feet and we applauded each other like a couple of old vaudevillians. Then we both looked around. The entire congregation was staring at us. In silence.

So total was the hush, that it was not just embarrassing, it was actually frightening. A chastened look spread over the little geisha's face and she slowly raised both tiny hands to her mouth, in horror. We had done something very, very wrong here, clearly, possibly unforgivable. With that final two-fisted piano chord still ringing out and the last 'lam bam boom!' still echoing around among the vast chandelier, the little pianist and I just looked at each other sheepishly and then down at the cream carpet, waiting to be hauled off and ritualistically fileted somewhere behind the building.

Idiot! What had I done? Would my guys be asked to leave? Be fired, even? But then one lone congregant, a short, tough-looking old bird, with buzz-cut white hair, a very exalted boss indeed as it turned out, stood up slowly and began almost soundlessly to clap, very formally, all alone. Then a lesser warlord got to his feet and followed suit, clapping a little louder.

And slowly, one by one, following a very strict order down the food chain, one after another of the audience got up and applauded with gathering enthusiasm and wider and wider grins until the whole three-button assembly was on its feet clapping and cheering. We had dodged the bullet. Or the *hara kiri* blade. The two of us bowed and bowed and I went over to my greatly relieved accompanist and raised her tiny fist in the air, little champ, to even louder roars of approval from the beaming consensus. The white-haired little Mr. Big had saved everyone's face and bacon, by making us a hit. It was the timeless tactic of the General. A subordinate embarrasses you? Give him a medal. Make it look planned. And that was the start. After that, the further adventures of the Goofy Gaijin became a corporate staple over our daily liquored-up Creative Meetings, quote unquote. Our social calendar was packed. We would go out every night to a different joint and I'd attack the Elvis/Little Richard/Jerry Lee songbooks with varying degrees of success and outrage and in the process would eat extremely well and expensively, boss's treat, feast upon indescribable feast, until one morning I looked down at my oddly pregnant form and realized that every single mouthful of every single banquet was still in there, and going nowhere. I had not shat in a week.

It was the food, you see. My digestive tract was entirely unused to product of this ilk. I was currently playing host to an anaconda of *materiel* that my stunned gut wished to not pass through *just yet*, because it was simply too fascinating. It contained items never before seen in these parts. Do you have any idea what they *eat* in Japan? Those with the serious dough, I mean, the ones with the kneeling geishas and the monogrammed malts and the wacky budgets?

Menu Item: Tofu 'Marquis de Sade'.

A very large pot of clear, steaming-hot broth is placed on a table before a circle of connoisseurs like oneself and their attendant geishae. A dish of tofu cubes is placed to one side of the pot, to the other side of it a glass bowl of tiny live fishes, swimming around. Geisha chopsticks are raised and at the ready, speed and timing being of the essence in this dish. The tofu cubes are dumped into the steaming soup. The live little fishes are tossed in right after them. The fish freak because the soup is murderously hot. They see the cubes of cool tofu and, quick as a flash, burrow into them to save their little lives. (Phew! That was a close one, eh, fellas?) But no! Geisha chopsticks dive into the cauldron like seabirds. They daintily snatch a tofu cube with a still-living wee slicket cowering timorous fishy inside it, and pop it into one's connoisseur gob, while it's still thrashing around daintily. One chews. One swallows. There is a muted round of polite applause.

One could go on. The list is long. Suffice it to say that this superb cruelty features little or no *roughage*. So, every night the inner serpent would put on a few more exotic pounds and tumesce ever more tightly against the retaining wall. After the first full week, so concrete-like was my unwelcome guest that I could spend entire mornings athwart the can and, red in the face, produce nary the teeniest soprano *peeep*.

But the banquets continued. Pretty soon a another week had gone by in this tumular fashion. By now, needless to say, I was performing only the later, *Fat* Elvis songbook, to keep it real. Something had to be done, and pronto. But here was the rub. My daily deejay gig with the thirteen models was up, and with it my free stint in the glass palace, dimpled masseuse, on-call physician and all. I was now sleeping cheap, on a hard tatami floor, no longer like a decorator samurai but a real one, in a little low-budget *ryokan* - a traditional inn - the real deal, with the sliding paper doors and bamboo drainpipes and little ladies scuttling around in hopi-coats with iron pots of green tea and - most important - *no flushing toilet.* There was just one of those entertaining holes in the floor with a bucket of water to slosh into it, like a beer chaser. We were in the grounds of the huge Akasaka temple, a place of national pilgrimage, a wooden giant with a roof so colossal they had built another, identical one on top of it, just in case you didn't believe it the first time. The whole *vérité* scenario was so cinematically authentic that nobody spoke English at all, not a word. The language-barrier task at hand was truly daunting, degree of difficulty? Off the charts. Marcel Marceau himself, the super-duper-mime, would walk away from this one.

"Dear little ladies. May I bring your attention to my enormous belly? No, I am not pregnant. This is actual shit. My bung-hole, you see, is totally bunged-up and I need to see a doctor, and pronto, to help me shift this Mount Fuji of umgawa. Otherwise, re-decoration, autumnal shades, flung dung, blah blah. Yadda yadda. Thank you. Thank you very much. Elvis is *stuck* in the building, know what I mean?

I put off the coming farce by phoning a young woman I knew who spoke very good English and I told her about the problem and how very ill I was starting to feel. I was. Very. You can imagine. But when she hung up, she sent me over a cure for diarrhea. Sweet arm-waving Jesus. This was worse than I thought. If I couldn't explain the awkward sitch to a hip young chick over the phone, how was I going to get it across to these polite old biddies in full drag who had looked aghast when I asked for the toilet by pointing to my ass and making fart noises?

And there was not a moment to lose, either. I really was starting to look quite jaundiced. I *was* the yellow peril.

Sitting there on my tatami, I started to panic. My body was beginning to poison itself. This was serious. In a few hours it would be daybreak and I must gather all the old girls together and explain it to them assembly style, so as to get their full attention and so that they could all help each other figure out exactly what the skinny gaijin with the big belly, the one who looked like an olive on a stick, was wind-milling about *this* time.

So, after they'd finished serving food next morning, while they were still clattering around in the kitchen, cleaning up after the usual icky breakfast of really stinky mackerel, cold dank seaweed, fatty lumps of left-over meat, pickled vegetables and the other options that should make all Japanese wake up screaming, I walked in and gathered them together in a line. There were six all told, all looking attentive but pushed for time, their little heads tilted quizzically to one side, as if to say, "We're listening. But make it snappy." So here we go, Muggins and the Munchkins. Showtime!

I opened the act by pulling up my tee-shirt and exposing the huge gut. They all took an involuntary step backwards, not having expected anything quite so intimate. I slapped the concrete balloon with both hands, one after the other, intending to demonstrate how rock solid it was, but causing them to raise their heads a little higher, like a row of chickens, waiting for me to play the rest of the tune. Oh dear. Maybe this was the wrong opening. But at least I had their full attention.

Then I started making eating gestures, shoveling imaginary food into my mouth with both hands, chewing loudly, then making 'it's getting bigger' gestures by moving my hands away from my belly while blowing out my cheeks. They all looked at each other as if to say, "Is he raving or is it just me?" Then they all looked back at me. This was the point in charades where somebody usually yells out, "Did you say this was a movie or a movie *star?*" But I forged ahead.

I mimed opening a door while holding my belly and looking pained. I squatted on my haunches, as over a hole, and strained, contorting my face livid, practically giving birth. Then I got up, made a big show of looking down the hole, looking up at them and shaking my head, as if to say 'there's nothing there' while looking very sad. Then I did the Greta Garbo, to show them *how* sad. You know the one. The Greta Garbo is where you put the back of your hand to your forehead and stare off camera, looking pained, like she did in *Camille*. It's a staple. Back of hand to forehead, stare off = I am sad. Trust me.

They looked at me with absolutely no expression on their faces, as if they were watching a raving lunatic demonstrate *exactly* how totally bat-shit he is. I did the whole thing again. Slapping belly, eating with two hands, belly getting bigger, toilet door, going in, squatting, straining, getting up again, looking down the hole. Seeing nothing. Shaking head. Looking sad. Greta Garbo. I looked at them in turn. They were just staring at me. I studied their faces for a glimmer of something, anything. There was nothing. No sale.

Then they all turned to each other and all started yammering at the same time, as if they all had completely different interpretations of this mating dance and were all making strong cases for their own take on it, shaking their heads, shrugging, jabbing the air with their fingers. How could they disagree so much? It all seemed so clear to me. Belly getting bigger, open toilet door, go in, squat, go red in the face, get up again, look down hole. See nothing. Shake head. Look sad. Greta Garbo.

But maybe that was the problem right there, the Garbo. I had often been in two minds about that one, I must say. I was never 100% sure

whether the full Greta looked like "I am sad" or "I am a *flaming* queen."
In which case, yes, maybe there were several other possible interpretations.

Suddenly, one of the old girls snapped me back to attention. She appeared to have had a blinding flash of insight, and ran over to me in order to check, gesture by gesture, if she'd got it right. They gathered around in a knot of focused concern, following her every movement. She did the eating thing. I nodded,
- Yes.
- *Hai,* she said to the girls.
- *Hai!* they all shouted back.
She blew out her cheeks and did the Big Belly gesture with her hands.
- Yes, I said.
- Hai, she said.
- Hai! They said back to her.
More eating.
- Yes.
- Hai
- Hai!
More puffed cheeks, more big belly.
- Yes.
- Hai.
- Hai!
The girls were leaning in, rapt, practically *on point* at this point. She opens the imaginary toilet door and squats.
- Yes.
- Hai.
- Hai!
Now even *I'm* getting excited. She strains, she grunts.
- Yes.
- Hai.
- Hai!
She gets up, moves away from the imaginary hole. Looks down it, looks up, gives it a dramatic pause, shakes her head.

- Yes.

- Hai.

- Hai!

Actually, that last part was brilliant. The pause before the shake? Pure Buster Keaton. Such timing. Damn, why didn't I think of that? I had *mime-envy.* I wanted another *go.* Or at least the chance to explain that I was unrehearsed, not at my best, etc.. Oh, well. Never mind. Next time. Stay in training. Stay focused. One day at a time. Can happen to the best.

Meanwhile, she's back in action. The audience is rooted to the spot. She squats. She strains. She grunts. She moves away. She turns around. She looks down. She looks up. The serious face. The full Buster Keaton. The pause. The pause. (Don't milk it, honey) The shake! BRAVO!!

- Yessss!

- Haiiiiiiii.

- Haiiiiiiiiii!

She's got it! They've got it! I'm saved! She gathers them all around her like a quarterback in a huddle, to make sure they all understand. She speed-gabbles some bullet-train Japanese at them. They all nod like crazy. Then she stands up straight, comes over to me, reaches up and puts her hand on my shoulder and yells at them a quick burst of something that sounds exactly as if she's saying...

"Sweet constipated Jesus, girls! This pot-bellied motherfucker's bung-hole is so bunged-up he hasn't shat in a fortnight. If we don't get it shifted, and pronto, he's gonna explode! Quick, let's get this shit bomb outa here before he goes off!"

And grabbing me by the hand, she walks me over to the door, we put on our shoes and we're out of there. The supporting cast stands in the doorway in an excited clump, waving bye-bye as Mama-San and Shit-Bomb plunge off at full shuffle through the temple grounds, already full of visitors at this hour, Mama San leading me by the hand as if I were the Helen Keller of constipation. What was she yelling to everybody? Step Aside? Gangway? Shit Bomb? Couldn't say exactly.

We wove across a main road through traffic, into a back alley, up a back stair and into a Chinese doctor's office. The place was packed, but everybody shut up when we burst in - well, you *would* - a big yellow gaijin with medicine ball under his shirt led by a squawking midget? The doctor was standing with his back to us by the desk. She dragged me to the front and tapped him on the shoulder, grabbing him by the lapel to get his attention as he turned around, He looked annoyed until he looked up and saw me, The Golem. Well, hey now.

She said something in a loud staccato to the goateed old boy. Then she turned to the audience and said it again, louder, as a kind of general announcement. There was a lot of nudging. They all stared at me. Nobody said anything. They all just gawked. Not that I could blame them. I was waiting for Buster Keaton to explain my ticklish predicament, discreetly, to the doc. But no. She just leaned against the wall and folded her arms theatrically.

The message was unmistakable. "Oh, boy. This I gotta see. This I wouldn't miss for a *pension.*"

Why, you eely old fish. You slippery old slope. You're going to make me act the whole thing out again, *for this lot?* Oh, well, why the fuck not? Showtime.

There was not a lot of response at first to The Belly, The Toilet Door, The Squat. The Strain. The Grunt. The Look Down The Hole. The Look Up Again. The Look Sad. The Pause, The Shake, The Greta Garbo. But sometime around the third run-through, coy Asian titters started to issue from the stalls. Then a chortle or two, a stifled honk and then peal of helpless giggles from two fat women leaning against each other just totally losing it. Thereafter, there was no holding back the flood. By the fifth go-around everybody was laughing so loud that nobody even noticed the guy who slid off his chair or the woman at the back just flat out barking.

And I must say I did get much better as the performances progressed. They started to get much more elaborate. By around the seventh matinée, I was spending whole minutes on just the straining part alone and the sadder the faces I pulled when looking up from the empty hole, the more I had them in stitches. Little Buster Keaton herself had long ago slid down the wall and, from a legs-splayed sitting posture, was making noises like a large bird I once heard in Australia.

She was still cackling to herself as we wove our way back through traffic to the little inn with a paper bag full of stuff I was variously instructed to either drink or shove, and she regaled the girls with the whole office visit, doing it over and over in the hallway, to bigger and bigger laughs, as I lay on my tatami, praying that these Hiroshima devices would work from both ends in tandem, as described.

And a hell of a description it had been, too, I have to admit. After I had finished my command performance, the old guy clearly hadn't laughed so much since medical school and, getting into the swing, he proceeded to act out The Cure with the same gusto that I'd brought to The Problem. To tell the truth, he got even bigger laughs than I did, but then I had softened them up pretty well for him, the lucky bastard.

What he needed to convey was that The Cure was to be a double-ender, as I mentioned, part pie-hole, part ass-hole, the critical element being the timely co-ordination of the two extremities. And it was here that he pulled off the show-stopper. He explained very easily that I had to take some pills and wait an hour. But then came the business at the, um, business end.

After waiting an hour, I was to shove a huge suppository up the old sphincter and then wait fifteen more minutes before Armageddon, the hilarious detail being that I must hold it in there for the full fifteen, and that it would be *very painful to do so*, because by this point, if his timing was right, the whole shebang would be on the move, roaring to get out and the suppository would remove the only cork that was holding it back.

He stuck his ass way out, then stuck his thumb out like a hitch-hiker and with a big sweeping motion, jammed it up his butt, with a loud "HUP!" There were cheers. Then he walked around like a duck on a hotplate, pulling some of the funniest faces you've ever seen outside of a monkey house, while ticking off fifteen big ones on his imaginary watch. The crowd went wild. They were close to wetting themselves some of them, as he, too, caught the mime bug and just milked it, waddling around pulling expressions of pain so hilarious, you would have sworn he started his medical career in the circus.

I was a bit pissed off to be honest. I felt like pulling rank. Hey, buddy, there's only *one* laughingstock around here and that's *me*, OK?

As Buster and I left the premises it was like being dragged away from a great party. Several of the patients followed us out onto the back stairs and yelled "HUP!" and jammed their thumbs in the air and fell about. It was possibly the best doctor visit in memory.

Long story short, I did all as instructed and barely made it into the toilet still continent. At exactly 15 mins and counting, the first Chinese fusillade rattled the paper walls, causing ladylike applause nearby and a round of ironic cheers in the distant kitchen. I was in there for a good half hour before it was all over and my sparrow's nest was rid of it's cuckoo. I tried to get up but couldn't. My knees were numb, both feet had fallen asleep and I was so light headed, I just pitched over sideways and lay there, hurting and laughing, having given birth to fourteen feasts, a pile of shrapnel and what felt like a set of nesting tables.

When I did finally emerge, showered, soaped, talcum-powdered, bath-robed and dizzy, I was greeted by an honor-guard of bowing and beaming mother-figures bearing little cups of tea and plum brandy and sake with tiny cakes in as many bright colors as the Sunday-best kimonos they had all donned sweetly, wittily, for the occasion. There was much laughter, sweetly embarrassing mime and many small hands over giggly lipsticky mouths.

I checked out the following morning, poste-haste and postpartum. And even after a big special-treat non-Japanese breakfast of eggs and toast, I was still so light on my feet that I felt like I might just float away over the roofing extravaganza next door.

On the threshold there was a lot of cheek kissing, and bowing, and little candies being shoved into my coat pockets as I slowly disengaged and bowed my way backwards into the temple crowd, then turned and headed for the subway station. But I hadn't gone many steps when I heard my name called and turned around as the whole little posse at the door jabbed their thumbs in the air and yelled "HUP"

OK, you got me, you silly bastards. I waved and left. Language barrier? What language barrier? Language barrier my sore ass.

NOTHING. BUT MONEY.

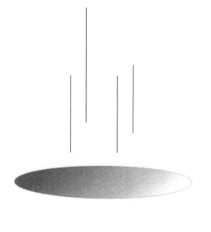

LAS VEGAS

There we were outside Las Vegas, the three of us recovering from another fine mess. We were standing around in the desert at high noon, bare-headed, sinking into the melting macadam of the local commuter airstrip, three rubes with one hangover, waiting to be flown out to the Grand Canyon to lunch with a bunch of Genuine Indians, quote unquote. We had taken so many aspirins we could not feel our hands. There were no dark glasses dark enough. We were swaying visibly, waiting for the little six-seater plane that would get us out of there and take our minds off the money we'd lost the night before.

We had dropped a very large part of our very small fortunes on a Sure Thing. Somebody knew somebody who had been informed that the unbeatable Mike Tyson, Undisputed Heavyweight Champion of the Entire World, was about to get his ass kicked. Unfortunately, they had not informed the referee.

Our fighter was named Razor Ruddick, a near giant from Canada, and he was doing OK for several rounds, considering the fact that he was in the ring with something barely human, and the usual ringside choir of armed pimps and squealing implants was cheering him on. Clearly he was *their* guy, too, and they had clearly bet pretty large on him, an encouraging sign. The three of us were starting to count our chickens. But then The Beast hit him with one of his patented head-removers and the ref stopped the fight, just like that. One punch. Our guy didn't even go down, he just wobbled a bit and appeared puzzled, as if looking around for the truck that hit him. But it was over.

The gangsters nearly exploded, all roaring, "Fix! Fix!" and lurching towards the ring like dancing bears with expensive watches, swinging at anybody within radius, including each other. Tyson scuttled out of there like a rat up a drainpipe and he was upstairs in his suite, showered, talcum-powdered and playing doctor with a few local beauty queens, before the much better *after*-fight was even getting into full swing, all to no point, of course. It was all over and our money was gone.

When enough large black men had been subdued by enough even larger black men in uniform, we slunk off to the blackjack tables to see if we were any luckier at cards than we were at prizefights. We were not. Ditto at dice. So at around three in the morning we threw in the towel and went back to what we knew we were good at - drinking ourselves stupid because broke.

And here we were, the following noon, on the melting runway, looking like we'd been carved badly out of week-old Spam.

Suddenly, out of the sun, like a migraine, a flashing metal streak of an airplane appeared above us and executed an elegantly swooping curve before touching down neatly into the puddle of liquid heat on the runway in front of us. It swooshed towards us smartly and parked center stage, after executing a cute little tail-swing to present its most attractive side in profile. The prop stopped and it just sat there, glinting. This was not our plane. No. This was not the specie of bone-shaker that ferries losers like us out to the Grand Canyon to eat lunch with a bunch of Genuine Indians, quote unquote. This was from another world entirely, from another time. This was possibly the most beautiful moving object I have ever seen, present company excepted.

It was an art-deco silver bullet with wings. It had long rows of little rivets all polished flush with it's shiny silver skin, like an old Cartier timepiece, as aerodynamic and fluid as a slim female nude, cast in platinum, glinting on a coffee table in a Humphrey Bogart movie in nineteen thirty something. We three stooges just stared at it and then at each other, each mouthing a silent 'wow'. Nothing happened for a while, apart from the staring and the tick-tick-ticking of its engine as it cooled down in the heat of the desert. Then a little round silver door was thrown open in the side of it.

What emerged were two very long legs tailored expensively in pale gray flannel with a shiny black cowboy boot on the end of each one. They swung there for a while, and then their owner slid the rest of his long frame out of the aperture and planted his boots onto the runway while he reached back inside for a black cowboy hat of the stiff Stetson variety and a pair of hand-tooled saddlebags in brown leather. He put the saddlebags over his shoulder and the black hat on his head. Then he closed the door and locked it and turned around to face us for the first time.

If you've ever seen James Coburn in *The Magnificent Seven,* imagine him in a pale gray bespoke Dallas suit with black trim, black boots, black shades and a black ten-gallon hat, and you've got the picture.

He loped over towards us lankily and unhurriedly, just like James Coburn, but for real, a tall tan dandy, a grey-haired, middle-aged, long drink of water, no doubt pegging us three bloodshot pot-heads for the cleaned-out big-city bozos we were. On his way over, he looked back a couple of times at the art-piece he had just swooped down in so stylishly from on high.

He mosied all the way over to us to check the local time, and seemed genuinely surprised that one of us actually knew it. He stood there for a moment, checking out one last time the *machina* that he was the *deus ex* of and I ventured to address the tailored god.

"Beautiful plane," I ventured.

"Yeah," he said in a deep drawl, nodding at it slowly, "Yeah. Ain't it?"

"Is it yours?" I asked, pointlessly.

"No. Uh uh. No, it's not."

"Where did you fly in from?"

"Aspen, Colorado."

"Nice," I said, the other two stooges nodding in agreement.

"You have a place in Aspen?"

"No. Uh uh. No I don't."

"So your home is here, then."

"No. Uh uh. No it's not."

"So. Er... where will you be flying to from here?"

"Austin, Texas," he said.

"Nice," I said, the other two stooges nodding in agreement.

"So, your home is in Austin, then?"

"No. Uh uh. No, it's not."

He turned to me slowly and spoke in a kindly, indulgent sort of way, as one might to slow child.

"Son, I don't have a place in Austin. Don't have one here in Vegas. Or in Aspen. Or anywhere. Don't own a house. And that is not my plane. I don't have *nothin'*. But money."

He let that hang there for a while in the sultry desert air, the man who had Nothing. But money. Then he grinned an affable sort of grin, which crinkled the attractive crow's-feet under the stylish shades. He touched his long, tan fingers to the brim of his stiff Stetson hat, then turned and loped away. Just like that. Just like James Coburn. But for real. The plump, hand-tooled saddlebags, presumably full of the money of which he had nothing but, were slung casually over his bespoke shoulder.

We three stooges turned and watched him walk away and disappear. Just. Like. That. He was swallowed up into the black noon shadow of an airstrip hanger. We could do nothing but stare at the wide black rectangle that had received him, and then at each other, shaking our heads and giving each other another silent-movie version of 'wow'. Then all three of us, as one, turned blearily away from our new role-model, the Unknowable, the Airborne Rumor, the Man who had Nothing. But money.

We turned and squinted together into the nauseatingly bright blue sky, as our own long-awaited conveyance announced its tardy - and very noisy - entrance out of the same blinding sun and hit the same spot on the shimmering tarmac. And that was as far as any similarities went with the winged dildo that was still going tick-tick-tick quietly in front of us.

Our own ragged-ass vehicle banged and bounced and wobbled its way down the runway, clattering towards us like some flying-circus clown, coughing and flapping and farting and belching smoke, a battered, clanking heap of aerial detritus, with all the art-deco grace of a three-legged dog on a rusty roller-skate.

LOST, STONED & NAKED

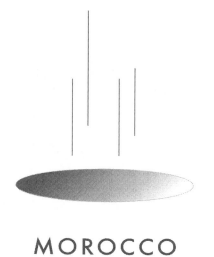

MOROCCO

My friend Michel's official job title is Designer and he's very good at it. But although this takes up a lot of his time, it's more of a hobby compared with his real career: Professional Frenchman.

He's the Frenchest guy in America. Hands down. It's a full-time gig and he's unsurpassed at every aspect of it - the slouch, the shrug, the stubble, the mumble, the shades, the cigarettes, the too-tight pants, and above all, *The Accent*.

Without exaggeration, he has the most exaggerated French accent ever seriously offered. It is a national treasure on two continents. It may wind up either in the Smithsonian or the Louvre. They both have their eye on it. But the point is that it's not a bad English accent, it's a *brilliant French one*. In fact, it's the perfect *derision* of everything that makes English English.

And it is only after listening to Michel's murderous send-up of the language of Shakespeare that one first notices that the cornerstone of all things Anglophone is, you have to admit, a bit sissy. It's the *th* sound. He does have a point.

Michel takes the *th* sound as a personal affront. He will not have it in his mouth. So for him, every little thing is a *leetle seeng* and every this, that or the other is a *zeece, zat or zee ozzair*. Michel has lived in America for thirty years and speaks English perfectly. And this is what makes him so fiendish, because you can't actually fault the bastard. And yet, every time he opens his mouth, what emerges is such an attack of militant Frenchness, that he makes Maurice Chevalier sound like Her Majesty the friggin' Queen.

- Say motherfucker, Michel.

- Moozair fookair.

- No. Motherfucker.

- Moozair fookair.

- Michel, if you can't say motherfucker, you can't stay in New York.

- Moozair fookair.

- See, in New York, 'motherfucker' is a *basic*, like...'and' or 'the'.

- Moozair fookair.

- You'll get your ass kicked, man. No. Wait. If you go up to some guy and say, hey *moozair-fookair*, he'll ask you for a croissant, *then he'll kick your ass.*

- Moozair-fookair.

- Have you ever considered Miami Beach? Now, *there's* a place you can say moozair fookair. They've even got French *bouncers* in Miami Beach. One more time. Motherfucker.

- Moozair-fookair.

- Miami Beach, man. I'm telling you. You'll love it. You'll get such a tan there, you can pass for Algerian.

- Meeyami Bitch?

- See! You're halfway there already.

I was thinking about Michel as I hurtled through the Moroccan desert one day, at blistering, sizzling high noon. How hot was it? It was hotter than Satan's *vagina*.

Michel and I were vaguely trying to find each other in vast, sun-baked Morocco and failing. Our 'strategy' for meeting up in this very big country seemed so simple at the time - possibly because it was hatched by two simpletons and is an example of why neither of us should be allowed in the military. This was in the days before mobile phones, when humans were not yet homing devices, and it was possible to lose contact with other people - such a luxury in retrospect - and you had to make something called 'a plan'. So quaint. We agreed on the route we would both take. We agreed on the hotels. We knew where we would stay in Marrakech, in Fez, in Casablanca and so on. So now all we had to do was leave each other notes at each place and we would hook up for sure. No problem. The problem was that neither of us knew *when* we would be *anywhere*. Michel began a few days ahead of me, on design business, moving with some purpose. I was there strictly on monkey business, so I was rather more aimless, unpredictable and easily distracted (a gypsy once drew similar conclusions from my palm).

But the main problem was that every time I arrived at one of the hotels there would be a note that read, no doubt in The Accent, "I was here. Where are you?" That's all. No mention of *when* he was here, or *where* he would be next. We were doomed. But it hardly mattered. Meeting had always been a maybe, and I was so tweaked on the local hashish that I may not have noticed him even if we had bumped into each other. And right now I was about to embark on one of my more monumental distractions.

I was driving across the desert on a road so straight it looked like one of those vanishing-point diagrams. It ran ahead of me in a perfect straight line and disappeared at the edge of a horizon so perfectly horizontal that I was actually thinking of calling the Flat Earth Society. To apologize.

Above was sky, below was sand. But by some fiendish coincidence, the sky was exactly the same sky-blue as my sky-blue rental car, a mind boggling perceptual conundrum, not helped by my serious hangover, Morocco being one of those countries where you never fully sober up from the shock of how drunk you can get for a dollar. So, with the sky-blue sky reflected in the sky-blue hood, I would have been hard pressed to tell you which way was up, zipping across this backdrop as fast as my little car would zip, tearing headlong into infinity, from geometry into the mystic.

This was the edge of the Sahara, as far as roads go in this moonscape quarter of Morocco. Up ahead, this flat sand would eventually start to undulate and swell into the heaving dry ocean that ate up a quarter of Africa and which terrifies me just to think about the infinite shifting treachery of it all. Off to my right there's a giant sandstorm blackening the sky in the distance, still a long way off, but approaching. Above my head, the sun is so bright it's invisible. And I have no water. And no map. And no clue.

I have no water because I forgot it. I was so caught up in renting the car in Marrakech, trying to read the paper in French - which was making my lips ache - and lingering over an espresso or two and a couple of really good croissants - buttery, but light and fluffy - so busy with all this really important stuff that I didn't attach much importance to *actual survival*.

When I did glance at the map and saw that where I was headed, there was nothing on it, no towns, no villages, not even a speck of fly shit, I quite honestly didn't believe it. I mean, there's always *something*, isn't there? I thought that the map was just too small or too vague to show all those great little roadside stands run by quirky characters in turbans who seem a little brusque at first but who turn out to have a heart of gold. It seemed a reasonable assumption. At the time. But I was wrong. The map was right. There's nothing. Whatsoever. Forever. And I'm thirsty.

But the map was moot anyway, because I'd forgotten that too. I'd been so busy forgetting the water that I omitted to remember it. So now I'm also lost, while dying of thirst.

And what's making me even thirstier is the fact that this blisteringly hot, dead-straight road is covered in rippling mirages. It looks like a long straight canal full of cool grape juice. How ironic. I glance at the fake Rolex. I've been on this road for ever. And the more bored I get with the pitiless straightness of it all, the more my eyes are drawn left and right into the wild, free-form desert on either side of it. The sand is not entirely flat or without incident, when you look closely. There are hillocks and hollows, wrinkles and ridges, dried-up rivulets, piles of rocks, skeletons of missing persons - exactly the kind of wilderness I came to Morocco for in the first place. I like deserts. I like walking through that sage-smelling furnace and watching the vultures as they circle so gracefully overhead, hoping you die. Deserts are beautiful. Well, they are if there's a car just out of frame with a tank full of gas. And water. And a map.

So I'm just *snorting* to turn off the road and plunge into it, to inhale it, instead of just whizzing through it in the safety of this sky-blue French tin can that I have revving so high it sounds like a pissed-off mosquito. But I'm afraid to. Oh sure, the sand looks pretty solid, and there are tire tracks here and there, but who knows what kind of quicksand lurks on either side of them? Maybe they're traps, lures laid by crafty Bedouin waiting behind a hill for you to disappear into a big hole so they can have your fake Rolex, the shifty bastards. But really, what if I *did* get stuck? I'm miles from anywhere in any direction, there's no traffic so there's no help, it's a hundred plus degrees out there, that huge black sandstorm is approaching, and I have no water. So I look longingly but keep driving. Then I see the headlights.

Way in the distance, coming towards me, some nutcase has his lights on full, even though it's the middle of the day. They are a long way off so it's a while before I see that they belong to a truck, a very big one, coming at me in its own personal dustbowl, swimming in its own mirage as if spilling mercury onto the road. It's barreling down the highway and belching smoke like some movie monster, but still far enough away that it's doing it all in silence. It's eerie and ghostlike and it's coming right down the middle of the road at me.

Now, that doesn't bother me at first, because I'm doing the same thing. When you're the only thing on the road for hours you start driving down the middle because you feel kinda stupid staying on 'your' side. A couple of times, earlier in the day, other cars have headed towards me doing the same thing, and we both slowed down, moved aside and let each other pass, while giving each other the cool-driver salute, you know, that quick little lift of the chin. All very civilized. "Bonjour. Au revoir. Merci." But each time there was barely enough road for us to pass without getting two wheels in the sand. And that was with just two cars. But this truck is massive. We're both going to have to slow down and do a very delicate little vehicular gavotte for both of us to stay even partially on solid ground. Well, that's what I'm thinking, anyway.

But the beast just keeps coming at full tilt, and now I can see that it's going really fast. The top speed of my little French poodle is about 70mph, and he's nearly that fast. So I slow down. But the truck doesn't. Not at all. It's already too close for comfort and going way too fast and

I can now see that it's enormous. That big dust-cloud all around it is only half dust. The other half is load.

It takes up the entire road. What the hell is he hauling? *Haystacks*? It cantilevers out crazily on both sides, barely held down by great flapping tarpaulins that are jouncing around like flailing sails in a sea-storm. And it's going flat out, just cannonballing towards me. There's no room for me whatsoever. It barely fits on the road itself!

Then the noise hits me. It's a bowel-loosening roar of a huge old diesel, red-lining at a good seventy miles per, in a ball of black smoke. And what's that thing waving out of the cab window? Oh, my God, it's an arm. It's a fat, hairy arm gesticulating wildly with a big fist at the end of it. Holy shit! He's waving me off the road! He's not going to stop at all. Then the roar suddenly ratchets up from bass to baritone. What? He's *accelerating*? He's trying to *fucking kill me?*

In seconds it's on top of me, God knows how many kinetic tons of roaring, honking, hurtling, flapping, belching, gesticulating, hairy Arab death coming straight for my narrow ass. At the last *possible* second, I wake up, unfreeze and swerve off the road – I'm still doing about forty – and plow into the desert with a great *Boosh!!!!* I slam through a wall of sand and pebbles that go *ratatatatatat* against the windshield. The truck misses me by a hairy arm's length and thunders by. As it passes, I yank my head around to catch a glimpse of him, Mohammed, the Unmerciful. I see his crazed mug glaring at me, eyes bulging with molten rage, still waving his fist and yelling some vile Islamic shit at me. "Infidel! Piece of sheet! I keel you! Die like dog!" (I think that was the gist of it) And he's gone.

Doynk! Doynk! Doynk! I'm lolloping around on my bucking blue pooch like a rodeo clown, holding on for dear life. Thank you very much for the - *doynk* - mouthful of sand and for sending me right off the - *doynk* - road in this French sardine can all across the - *doynk* - desert until we - *doynk* - get back onto the road again.

My heart is still doing the clog dance as I wrestle the little frog-mobile into a straight line on this melting licorice strip and fishtail away in the direction I was headed. Holy shit! Did you see that? Tried to kill me! Unbelievable! You…you…*moozair fookair!!!.*

I can barely believe I made it back onto the road again and that I'm in one piece. But the little car's still going. Gotta hand it to those goofy-talking French, they do make a spunky little conveyance, accent or no accent. I point the game little pastel poodle in the direction I was going before being so rudely interrupted by Mohammed the pig-molester.

A mile or so down the road I un-palpitate. I scooch around in my seat to regain my former equipoise and re-orient the buns for the long haul. I light up one of my Gauloises, those *really* stinky French cigarettes. I inhale that heady cocktail of Paris sewer that always has a calming effect on me. Then I redirect my formerly debonair gaze down that long lonesome highway that runs with unwavering precision into the distant… headlights?

Another one? Another drunken boatload of hairy A-rab road rage bearing down on me at whack-job speed with the horn and the flapping and the smoke and the… whoooaahh, here we go again! Swerve, swerve. Gangway girls, doynk doynk doynk. And there he goes, roaring by me, Omar the Odiferous. "Bastarrrd! Infidel! I keel you! Die like dog!" Vroooomm! Gone.

Such rude people! I seem to have stumbled upon the Moroccan Synchronized Roadkill team in convoy. All bad teeth and nose-hair. Over the next ten minutes or so, the little *pas de deux* is executed several times. But as soon as I catch a distant glimmer of headlight, I just glide right off the road, slicker than snot on a doorknob, and skitter across the sands with a growing sense of confidence, not to say actual pizzazz. In fact, it's all turning out pretty well, come to think of it. With every forced exit, I take wider loops into the sand. Soon I'm not even getting back on the road. I'm just driving parallel to it, waving at the murderous swine, and now that I know my place on the road-kill food-chain, they wave a Bedouin bonjour. We're pals now. We salute each other with good-natured badinage.

"Hi! How's your toothless, bearded hag of a wife, the cloven-footed whore? And the inbred kids? Marvelous. Carry on!"

And yes, I must say, this is more like it. Look, Ma, no road. I'm driving across the actual *Sahara* it's own bad self. Me! Just like I wanted to. And the little Renault doesn't get stuck at all, seems to like it in fact. The locals do have a nickname for this little car, *le dromadaire*, the camel. And now I can see why. It goes forever on one drink. And it's so light it just skims over the sand. I guess this is the *true* ship of the desert these days, now that it would cost you several bearded wives to buy a real camel. And these come in such fetching pastel shades, too. I suddenly feel not just secure but rather chic as well, in my little Parisian desert accessory in pale *bleu*.

So now I'm just bouncing along Bedouin-style, and the sand feels hard as rock, all perfectly safe. I'm puttering around hillocks, rolling over rills and driving down little dips and dells. This is the life, eh? Yes, I am aware that I'm in a hurry, that I have no water, and really should get a move on. But, it's all so exotic and cool that I can't, and anyway, I'm not actually *dying* of thirst...yet... *am* I?

At the end of this long straight endless highway, I'm hoping I might bump into Michel in Erfoud, a once-spectacular oasis with a romantic past but a threadbare present, in *serious* Sahara, where the camel trains used to set off, for a year of rhythmic cock-and-ball torture all the way to Timbuktu and back. But right now I'm into my unscheduled *Dimwit of Arabia* interlude, and Erfoud can wait. Call me romantic, but I just *must* drive deeper into this shimmering movie set this very minute. So, without further ado, I do. I turn and drive away from the safety of the road into the infinite.

And zat, as Michel would say, *eez where ze sheet 'eet ze fan.*

I drive deep into the desert without a care. Or a compass. Or water. I just go, in the direction of the gathering sandstorm. Yes, it is an evil-looking colossus and a profoundly scary force of nature and contact with it could prove fatal. But let's not allow that to spoil a perfectly lovely afternoon, shall we? It's still a long way off and I've been waiting for this moment for a long time, almost since I arrived.

I've been in Morocco a little over a week now and it's all been great. The morning of the day I arrived here, I was in Paris. It was January and so cold in Europe that there were pictures in the paper of the Pope throwing snowballs in the grounds of the Vatican. At whom, it didn't say. Muslims, possibly?

How cold was it in Paris? It was so cold in Paris that the flashers in the Bois de Boulogne were *describing themselves.*

I flew to Marrakech just to get warm. And the flight was cheap. But I landed in the middle of an Arabian wet dream, a legendary event - the 25th anniversary of King Hassan's reign, the most spectacular weekend in living memory, and it was all just dumb luck, the only kind of luck I've ever had, to be perfectly honest.

Marrakech is the jewel in the crown even without this special feature presentation. But now, with the King there and all his princes, princesses, wives, concubines, small furry mammals and God knows what other pleasures, it was off the charts. Right outside the medieval walls there were mind-boggling parades every day, right up to those gilded purple thermonuclear sunsets. The pride and joy of Morocco was showing off to the adoring people. The kingdom. The power. The glory. Waves of white horses with gold saddles, their cavalry officers in red robes and turbans, banners on lances, scimitars drawn, the whole nine yards. Brigades of black horses with hussars on them in gold cloaks, and lances with long red ribbons flying behind them, armies of camels, hundreds of drummers and those women who do that yodeling thing that scares the shit out of you. It's a terrifying sound. It's called ululation. But it's so fierce, I think it may have something to do with *ovulation.*

All day this mile-long medieval war-machine would go swirling around the ramparts, an endless parade of hand-stitched, gold-trimmed galloping leather and metal, showtime, from early afternoon until the sun would sink, the dogs bark, the parade pass and all of us be drunk on spectacle, drunk on history and just plain *drunk*, high on the smells and the sounds and the colors and the kind of *kif* that could make you cross-eyed.

But ever since it finally petered out and I saddled up the blue poodle and zoomed off through the big Marrakech stone gateway and away into the Atlas mountains, I've been waiting for one thing. The desert. The real desert, the rolling ocean, *The Great Emptiness,* as they call it here. I had some foolish vision of myself walking along the crests of huge white dunes under the stars. And here I was, finally, in the desert. OK, it wasn't my *Lawrence of Arabia* wet dream, but it was the real desert, endless and mysterious. And once in it, once far away from that road and driving slowly deeper into it, I was finally starting to experience something close to what scuba divers call 'the rapture of the deep'. You've heard of it, I'm sure. You drift. You lose track of time. You forget. You drown.

So, before getting too carried away, let's just take another gander at that sandstorm, shall we? Hmmm. Not so dread. Not yet. It's miles away. Couple of hours at least, I'd say. I've driven over a mile from the road by now, far enough that I can't see it any more. I figure I'll putter around out here for half an hour or so, then I'll have an hour on that straight road to Erfoud, ample time to beat the storm into the big oasis. Sure. No problem. By the time that sucker makes it to the road I'll be basting my ass in a warm hotel pool, looking up at the palm trees and the vultures wheeling overhead hoping I die, while I'm reading the latest note from the elusive French, telling me *exactly* where he no longer is.

I arrive at a pretty little spot surrounded by low dunes and flowering succulents, all very diorama, perfect for my wander into the wilderness and my communion with the spirits of the sands. So I stop the car and get out, listening to the pleasant tick-tick-tick of the cooling engine under the hot blue hood. I smell that giddy odor of roasted emptiness spiked with dead lizard. I look at the sandstorm again. Wow. It *is* pretty frightening. Up this close, it reaches what looks like a mile into the sky, a great dark wall, but arriving more slowly than I had previously thought. In fact, it's all so perfectly perfect right here, I'm just gonna stop worrying and smoke a big fat joint.

Now, since I'm hungry as well as thirsty at this point, haven't eaten for many hours in fact, one big hit and I'm toast. Plus, at this precise moment it does occur to me for the first time that maybe, now that you mention it, I might also be coming on to that rather large lump of hash I swallowed, oh, an hour or two ago, and, um, kinda forgot about? Oh, dear. Oh, well. Oh, who cares? How much brain do I need out here, anyway?

And this is great. Just what the witch-doctor ordered. Look at this scene, man. It's beautiful. It's... it's... it's really weird how, at moments like this, alone in some natural paradise, instead of wanting to tear off a sonnet, I just want to tear off my clothes. So I do, all of them, even the fake Rolex. Yeah, this is more like it, Sahib. Bare-ass. That's the ticket. Oh, and will you look at that car. Cute little thing. I didn't notice before, but it appears to be sculpted entirely out of marzipan. God, I really do have the raving munchies. Now, I must make sure to not lock the door accidentally as I close it on all my possessions. See! Pretty smart, huh? Gotta get up early in the equatorial a.m. to outfox the desert fox, eh? For it is I, none other, who now stands naked before you, Mustafa. And speaking of Mustafa, I simply mustafa pee. I'm bursting. I'll do it from the pinnacle of yon tawny hillock. Ah, and behold, here I am, atop it, naked master of all I survey. Watch me urinate. Whoooosh!!!! Urinate. I'm innate. We're all innate together. Look at me. Sheikh Rattle and Roll! I am a river to my people! Wheeeeeeeeee!!

Well, after more of that sort of gibberish, I calm down from the grass-and-hash double-whammy, and settle down into a happy little groove of lovey-dovey to all things visible and invisible and turn my bare self away from the marzipan to venture off ever deeper into the uncharted watercolor.

I set off naked towards the rearing black sandstorm which by now has swallowed up a good half of the sky with a wall of swirling black.

It's just so gigantic and tall and sky-swallowing. But it is still clearly, in my sharp-as-a-tack calculation, roughly a…a certain way off.

I must have looked *certifiable* as I meandered off on my walking tour of Oblivia, whistling a tune and loving all things equally. Brother Scorpion, Sister Beetle. But after a very long, un-timed walkabout, I finally looked at the blank spot on my wrist where the fake Rolex no longer was, and figured it was time. So I point my little pointer back towards safety and everything I own.

The storm wall was finally getting a bit too sky-scrapingly close for dilly-dallying. It was a wee touch of the old darkness at noon. I could even feel on my bare skin the first goose-bumpy ruffles of the breeze that had crossed so many miles and was now hauling so many tons of airborne, murderous *materiel* that could sandblast my butt right off my pelvis.

I jogged back happily, stoned and naked, lost and stupid, the willy going wibble wobble as I ran up to the tops of the little soft baby dunes and somersaulted ass-over-tit, down the other side, all the way back to the little hillock where I had left my little car. I can't remember ever feeling quite so good, so completely drained of everything bad, and simply – as corny as it sounds – cleansed somehow by this genuinely moving communion with something so poetically enormous. Even sober, I'm sure I would have found it immensely emotional. As it was, I crested the top of that last little hill in a state of extraordinarily blissful calm. There in the distance was the road. And here in front of me, my trusty little car was......gone.

It was gone. *My little car was gone!* It wasn't there.

I don't know what a heart attack feels like, and I have never fainted, blacked out, had an epileptic seizure, or a near-fatal embolism. So I can't be sure about this, but I think that I had all of the above at once. And I can't report this with absolute assurance, either, but I think I might have ever-so-slightly *shat.*

My car was gone. Who took it? My little poodle from Paris was wagging its tinny tail somewhere else. Who took it? My sole means of egress from this theater of death is missing. There is nothing here remotely redolent of my former vehicle, not a trace or smell or spoor. Even the tracks of its arrival and departure have been erased by the accelerating wind. *I'm gonna die!* A naked man may not survive a full-on jet-engine sandstorm. I saw that on a National Geographic Special.

And this is not even the worst of it. Gone with my car is everything I own, not the least of which is everything that I am currently not wearing. Who took it? I am totally naked, my body innocent of even a watch. It begins to soak in, slowly, the totality of what I am without. Not just all my clothes, but all my money, my credit cards, my passport, every single form of ID. I am a non-person. Even worse, I am a naked non-person. *I am the ultimate have-not.*

Who took it?

Standing here on my hillock, which rhymes with *stupid friggin' pillock* the enormity of it begins to sink in. I raise my hands slowly to my temples like Gloria Swanson, and discover that I do still have one thing left. My sunglasses. Oh joy. Oh, thank you, Dear Lord and Fake Ralph Lauren. Oh, how very important it is to me at this moment to know that while impersonating the dimmest prick on the planet, I still exude style.

Who took my car? Who would do such a thing? How could this be possible? Nobody followed me here. Well, I wasn't looking back to see if anybody did. But then why would I? The road was empty when I turned away from it to connect with my inner retard. Could some guys have been driving down the road far behind me and noticed me turning off and decided to follow? Yes, of course they could. What could be an easier score than to follow the tire tracks of a lost moron in a desert? Imagine rolling up to find, unattended, a brand new sky-blue rental full of clothes, money, credit-cards, passport, fake Rolex, and with keys thoughtfully left in the ignition? Do they wonder, I wonder, where the owner is, and what sort of death they may be condemning him to if they steal it? Do they *fook!*

I scan the sands for any plume of dust. But there is nothing. I can't even see any tracks. The quickly gathering gale has now blown sand over everything. My car is lost without a trace. And so, too, maybe, am I?

In about ten minutes, the willy won't be going wibble wobble any more. It will be blown off, along with my face and the rest of the meat on my bones, If anyone ever finds me - and there's no reason why anyone should, out here in a place that's not even a place - they'll find a blow-torched skeleton picked clean by little desert critters. Brother Scorpion. Sister Beetle.

I have to make the worst decision of my life, although it's no decision at all. I have to turn away from here and run to the road, naked, in fake Ralph Lauren shades. I don't have any time to think about it, either.

I can feel the sand whipping at my skin. I turn around and look up with horror at the planet-sized tsunami that is now rearing up over me like the cobra god of Bedouin vengeance, only minutes away from engulfing me and rendering all decisions moot.

I'm openly sobbing with fear as I run down the sand dune and up the sand dune next to it, because the next one is slightly higher and will give me a better view of the road. I'm now stone-cold sober. Through my tears I can barely make out a few cars a couple of miles away zooming along the distant road, happy specks full of happy people, none of whom ever got seized by bizarre primal urges to pull suicidal stunts that seemed like so much fun - at the time. And they are *so far away*. Even at a thirsty trot - and I'm now dying of thirst - it will be touch and go to get there ahead of the sandstorm. And of course, as the sandstorm gets closer, there will be no traffic at all on the road. Drivers in the desert are not that stupid. Well, with one exception they're not. My face buried in my hands, reluctant even to look ahead, I take the first fateful steps down the side of the sand-hill on my run to the road to throw myself on the mercy of strangers, *totally naked*. I look down to see where I'm placing my bare feet. And there, below me... is my car.

Right there where I left it, my lovely little escape-module carved out of sky-blue Parisian marzipan and looking even more coquettish than usual. There it sits, my low-swinging sweet chariot, waiting for to carry me home. Allah is merciful. Today, Allah is extremely merciful to an extremely fortunate fuckwit. I damn near ran away from that car, not knowing it was there.

Well, I wasn't *far* wrong, was I? Just one dune wrong. Come on, guys. A mere quibble. I'm never far wrong, you see. And I didn't lose my cool at all. Ahem.

I run down the dune, get in the car, place naked butt on *very* hot seat. Yaahhh! Turn on the ignition, car starts, vive La France, tally ho, step on the gas gently, start to move forward gingerly, slowly around the little hill, prior to flying at full tilt towards the road like shit off a shovel. And *Fffppttt*. Oh. We appear to be stuck.

I get out of the car. Oh boy, we're stuck, alright. One of the front wheels is up to its axle in sand. Bugger. Gotta think fast. The wind is rising. The sand is now really pelting. I have no shovel, no nothing. The only tool I have is attached to me. And it's shrinking.

Oddly enough, one of the few useful skills I have is digging a car out of sand, thanks to many drunken weekends at the beach. If I weren't in such a screaming hurry, I'd be calm. I know I can do this. But can I do it fast enough? I get on my knees and dig out behind the stuck wheel with my bare hands, sling a pile of pebbles in the hole, something to give us a little purchase, then I slide in very gingerly behind the wheel, and I start her up, and as gently as I know how, tightening my sphincter until it almost whistles, I slip her in reverse, ease the clutch, up she comes and...down she goes.

But this time she goes *all the way down*. Oh, sweet doomed Jesus. I get out of the car and I'm confronted with a full-on genuine desert catastrophe.

All four wheels are now deep in the sand. And I am deep in the shit. The whole area was apparently just a tease, an ironic veneer of hard surface, under which there is a quagmire of talcum powder. I'm galvanized into action. I'm a dervish, a human blur. The sand-storm is now starting to really hammer at my skin. I should stop and put on some clothes but I don't dare waste a precious second. I throw open the doors and hurl everything out of the car to make it lighter. I run off in all directions, pulling up plants and roots and scrounging every loose item of anything lying around, twigs, rocks, anything I can see. I run around like a fool, digging and uprooting, hunting and gathering, until I have great piles of detritus heaped everywhere around the car. Now I'm getting dangerously thirsty. I'm deeply dehydrated, but what am I gonna do, stand on my head and piss in my mouth? Maybe later.

I cram all the stuff I've collected near all the wheels. There are four massive piles of crap. I dive in under the car. It's blazing hot under here and as I start to sweep with my arms further and further under the vehicle, I begin to scrape my bare back on the hot metal plates and gash it on all kinds of jagged nuts and bolts. It's a blood-bath under here. I should stop and put on a shirt, but I'm afraid to stop. I'm sobbing loudly with effort and self-pity. I'm scared stiff. I'm a self-hating, naked, blood-encrusted, sobbing shithead. In fake Ralph Lauren shades.

I finally stand upright and get absolutely slammed by the storm. I'm right in it now. It's just a screaming sheet of howling sharp nails shredding my bleeding back, and black as night. But I feel rather foolishly pleased with myself. The car is now standing in a huge bowl, all dug out by my own bleeding hands, with long herbaceous tracks extending backwards from each wheel like organic vapor trails. I resist the urge to photograph it for some art magazine. But I can now feel blood running down my back and into my ass crack (a not-unpleasant feeling, since you ask).

Gingerly, with the very utmost of ginger, I slither in and fire her up. Stately as a galleon, she eases backwards along her ad-hoc vernacular rails and onto terra firma. As my mother used to say, 'the more firmer, the less terror.' I exhale. I disembark, run around, recover my raiment, lug my luggage, and drive away, only occasionally letting out a blood-curdling shriek as my scraped-off skin smacks against the burning seat-back.

An hour later I'm lying on a big table in little hospital. It's late afternoon, shafts of golden nostalgia stream through the windows onto my impressive wounds. I could not put on a shirt, because of all the blood and the sand on my back. So when I walked in, I must have looked like the victim of a flogging, or some other arcane branch of sexual entertainment. The doctor was impressed.

- My God. Who did this to you?
- Er...nobody.
- You did this to yourself? What sort of a pervert are you?
- Er...well...
- Well, whatever sort, we can treat you.
- For my perversion?
- For your *back*.
- Oh.

He took perfect care of my shredded flesh with what looked like very expensive ointments and dressings. I was undeserving, and felt even more guilty when he refused all payment. A desert prince.

His assistant, however, was less courtly. During the long gentle treatment, I became engaged in conversation with him. Abdul the Sardonic.

- You should have driven a *dromadaire,* my foolish friend.
- I *was* driving a *dromadaire.*
- If you can call that driving.
- I drive pretty well.
- So, why are you here?
- Well, how would you drive it?
- Not like you obviously.
- It was unavoidable.

- If *you* were driving, yes. It was.

They can keep this up for hours, the Berbers. Dueling insults is an Olympic event in Morocco. Pretty soon the doc and I were just laughing. I stood no chance. So I just drifted off, listening to him, thinking back. I had not been very far wrong. One dune wrong, that's all. But I had almost walked away naked from every trace of identity. A stark naked young white man in fancy sunglasses suddenly appearing, like a mirage, to some pitiless Sahara scavengers, many miles from anywhere, on a road going from nowhere to nowhere else. What a score. A gift. A toy. Never heard from again. One dune wrong.

As it happened, my fate was not pitiless. Just pitiful. And comical. Face down on a slab in a hospital, cleaned, disinfected, covered in goo, laughed at and teased by my new scourge, Abdul the Sarcastic.

But there was method to his sarcasm as he swung the conversation around to asking why I was driving in such a nondescript shit-hole, and thence to informing me where I *should* have been driving, (if you can call that driving) According to Abdul, I should have been driving to The White Dunes.

- Whu? What? *The White Dunes?* (Had he read my mind?)

- These white dunes, are they far?

- They can be reached by nightfall.

- Are they beautiful?

- Like the breasts of virgins.

- And they're really white?

- White as that toilet bowl.

- *That* lovely? And how would I find them?

- You would not.

- Why can't I drive there myself?

- Why are you in hospital?

Outside in the parking lot, we're both standing there in white floor-length djalabis, mine bought from the hospital shop as the only practical way to accommodate all my bandages. It's the first time I've worn a full-length dress and I feel naked without the handbag and the high heels. I share a Gauloise with Abdul the Pitchman as he runs the deal down. If I will give him a few Drachmas and my car keys and let him drive me, he will take me to spend the night at the fabulous white dunes.

- Where will we sleep?

- A surprise.

- Why must *you* drive?

- The route is dangerous, there are no roads, the white dunes are
  two hours from here, straight into the desert. I am one of the few
  who know the way, and the last few miles will be in twilight, even if
  we were to leave now. And first we will have to buy food for ourselves
  And for my friends.

- Friends?

- They live there.

- In what?

- A surprise.

Well, well. Here we go again. Out of the frying pan. I think about Michel. "I am here. Where are you?" Well, old pal, I'm contemplating the possibility of handing over my car to an unknown Arab. He and I are to set off deep into the featureless Sahara for a two hour drive into the unknown, to arrive - at night, no less - in a place where his friends are waiting. What would you do?

The upside is an adventure of the type I drool over, a poetic journey into the heart of a desert paradise. I picture myself striding along the summits of huge, rolling white waves, under a mantle of stars adrift in the great arching vault of nocturnal, nomadic Africa. The night air is redolent of frankincense and jasmine and alive with the song of a solitary nightingale and the call of distant drums. Ahem.

Then there's the downside. I am pecked to death by buzzards on a garbage dump on the far side of town. I have been repeatedly gang-raped by the same bunch of lunatics who are now far away from here, selling my passport and credit cards, spending my cash and driving around honking the horn of my stolen car. On the hood, wired to the word *Renault*, is a new hood ornament that looks strangely familiar. At every bump in the road, it goes wibble wobble, wibble wobble.

I look at Abdul. He is smiling at me. Why? In happy anticipation at the joy that awaits me in the desert, or… Oh, what the hell. I throw him the keys. I also surreptitiously take my knife out of my bag and slip it into my belt.

*   *   *   *

Well, I'll say one thing for the dude. He sure knows how to drive on sand. After an hour's full-tilt zoom into the approaching evening, we have been through every possible sand hazard and he's taken them all with flying colors, turning to me at every vanquished obstacle, slapping the dashboard and yelling *"Dromadaire!"* I even get the distinct sensation that the high-revving poodle is digging it all, too. At dried-up rivers, Abdul has slid us expertly down one side and roared up the other, at grades I would never have attempted, angles so acute that all my loose clothes have flown from the back seat onto the windshield and then back again as we howled up the other side. Long stretches of soft sand I would never even dare enter, he has flown over as if we were on skis. The trick, which he never tires of rubbing in, is to constantly throw the wheel back and forth so that the tires slalom over the surface and you dance over it like a water-bug. Wow. I'm deeply impressed. In fact, if we were to turn back right now and never make it to the white dunes, I would consider it the thrill of a lifetime, just to be driven by him. I'm completely in his hands.

Now, most of the time that's a good feeling. Occasionally, however, I pat my knife.

We talk. He's educated. We discuss a few writers, a few movies. We talk about the desert, other deserts, American deserts. The more we talk, the more I like him, but I'm never quite relaxed.

How he finds his way is beyond me. He will, for instance, suddenly make a sharp course correction in the middle of nowhere, then point out some micro feature that prompted it, invisible to all but the initiated.

The desert is slowly becoming more contoured and rolling and dramatic. Finally, after a long uphill slope, he stops the car on the edge of an enormous plateau that seems to float above the rest of the desert. There is nothing here, nothing at all for as many flat miles as we can see. There's a sense of being on top of the world here. We are above everything. But why did we stop? He turns to me.

 - Get out.

 - What?

 - Get out, *please.*

 - You first.

He smiles an ironic smile and gets out. I slip my knife into my hand, behind my back. Then I get out. I look around. Nothing. This would be the ideal place to do it, whatever he's going to do to me. My heart lurches into a canter.

 - Get down on your knees.

 - What?

 - Do it.

 - Why?

 - Do it, *please.*

 - *You* do it.

He gets down on his hands and knees, grinning to himself. My God, must he smile like that? Is he gonna get medieval on my ass? Is this some antique Bedouin murder ritual? Do we start knifing each other from a kneeling position? Right now I'll stab him if he so much as looks at me. The keys are still in the car. I edge back towards it, slowly. He starts scratching around in the sand, laughing to himself. Oh, dear God, must he keep chuckling? He's a bona fide whack job, unless he's just laughing at the ease with which he lured me out here to where even the vultures can't find their way home. While I'm inwardly yammering, he suddenly jumps up and runs at me. It's so sudden, I can't even get my knife into my hand in time. He sticks something up into my face. I almost yelp with fear.

 - *Look!*

- *Whaa?*
- Look, Alan. See!

I look. It's a fossil. A trilobite, of some sort. A fossilized snail. Rather pretty. He's laughing at me now, openly. He's all teeth. He looks like a total maniac, a thrill-killer, a nut.

- Give me your knife.
- What knife?
- The knife you're holding behind you back. Give it.
- No.
- OK. Give it, *please.*

He roars with glee. Now he's hugely amused. I'm terrified.

- OK, Alan. Keep your little knife. I have knife.

He puts his hand into his white djalabi and, with a big flourish, pulls out his own knife. Abdul's knife is a foot long, a murderous thing, a true weapon. My knife is one of those Swiss Army things for getting splinters out, whittling sticks and opening wine-bottles. Abdul, with his dagger raised, looks like Saladdin, scourge of the Crusaders. Me? I look like Martha Stewart.

- OK. What do you want, Abdul?
- You don't get it, do you, Alan?

Oh, I get it alright, you son of a bitch. This is where I get offed, fileted with that evil-looking thing and served with a small side order of cous-cous. I can see that blade going through me like butter. I just wish I had bit more serious Martha artillery with me, you bastard. If I could just get your balls into a Cuisinart, I'd show you what pain is, you grinning fucker.

He holds up the fossil in front of my face, like a final sacrament, a last rite, a thing one does in these parts before plunging the cold steel into your gut.

You don't get it, do you? This thing is a *sea* thing. These are *all* sea things, all of them. All of this (he sweeps his arms around dramatically indicating the limitless plateau) all of this, millions of years ago, was the sea. At the top of the world, we are standing on the bottom of the ocean. Is it not fantastic, Alan? Is it not?

He giggles, drops down onto his knees and starts digging in earnest with his back to me, hacking away with his great, gleaming stabbing machine. I stand there, watching him blankly for a few long moments of comprehension. Then I sink down onto my own stupid knees, and start jabbing away wearily, sheepishly, with my own pathetic kitchen-implement. After a few minutes we have both dug up scores of these elegant, eloquent spirals, tossing the best ones to each other as we do.

The tension is all drained out of me. It's been a long day. I just can't worry any more. He could have cut my throat on the outskirts of town. I feel like a jerk. I can barely look him in the face.

Gunning across the huge plateau as fast as the little car will gun, racing across the floor of an ancient ocean that is now high up in the air, in a lilac twilight I cannot even begin to describe, stars appearing, no moon, the ground turning silver beneath us and a mile-long rooster-tail of tinsel and phosphorescence billowing behind us, I occasionally look down at the impossible sea thing in my foolish palm. Abdul is singing, happy as a lark. Me, I'm just quietly thinking to myself, 'Is it not fantastic, Alan? Is it not?'

Soon the darkness starts to come on fast and when Abdul puts on the headlights, the sense of floating high above the world, untethered, disconnected from it, becomes even more surreal. The feeling of altitude is further enhanced by the slow emergence, in the distance ahead of us, of banks of white cloud that the high plain seems to rise above. It is only as we get closer to them, as the sky darkens and the contrast between the pale clouds and the navy blue night becomes more acute, that I realize that these are not clouds. We slow down as we approach the far rim of our darkling plain and come to a halt right at the dizzy edge. We get out of the car and my pulse ramps up into a gallop as I realize what it is I am looking at. These are not clouds at all. These are the white dunes.

We are looking out across an ocean of huge white waves all frozen in mid-swell, disappearing into the roiling dark eternity out there in the direction of camel-trains and Timbuktu and the Great Emptiness itself. They are enormous. Endless. Glowing. Bright white. They catch the last vibration of disappearing daylight and the first hint of coming starlight and gleam from without as they seem to glow from within. They are silver-white mountains of powdered diamond, radiating a white inner light, a lava-flow of sculpted platinum. Huge. They go on forever. They shine nearly as brightly as the stars that light them, stars which are now appearing in their millions. I turn and look behind us in the direction of our tire tracks across that featureless Waiting-For-Godot plain we just crossed. It is almost black in that direction. I turn back to the white dunes below and ahead of us. It is a rolling sea of light. You could read a book by it.

- Did I not promise you a miracle, my friend?
- Yes, Abdul. You did.
- Young girls' breasts I said.
- Yes. And toilet bowls.
- To see is to believe.
- No. To see is to *not* believe.

Abdul rolls us carefully over the lip of the bluff and points out our final destination. It's a tiny little square dot at the foot of a massive dune.

- What *is* that, Abdul?
- It is a café.

Ah. Well, of course it is. As he slithers us skillfully down the side of the high plateau and into the shining, rolling sea of white sand, agoraphobia starts to overtake awe. From above, the dunes looked big, but from down here at the foot of them, craning your neck to look up at their crests from below, it is something else entirely. These are literally small mountains of powder, not really solid, not really still. Close up, driving alongside a dune, too close for comfort, you can look way up and see many subtle wave patterns made by endless avalanches down the sides, sides that are alarmingly steep, sometimes almost vertical. They really do look like frozen breakers about to break right over you. I have to keep reassuring myself that they will not suddenly collapse and drown us under a slagheap of stardust.

I try to stay cool long enough for us to skirt the last teetering wave and arrive at our impossible destination. Up close, that little square dot turns out to be quite a big building, the size of a generous two-story house, a dark rectangle of adobe with a flat roof and with a couple of tiny windows that are shuttered, but which have chinks of warm light squeezing through little slats in the wood. Somebody is home, here in the middle of the moon. Smoke is curling up from a chimney somewhere and, like everything else around here, is illuminated by the glow from the starlit dunes and the by stars themselves. It is a moonless night, but the wattage from the Milky Way, amplified by the white sand, is casting sharp black shadows all around. It's hard to believe. So is the sign painted on the side of the building. 'Café.' Well, of course. If that were not enough, there are also, leaning up against the wall, big as life, two sets of skis.

- Skis, Abdul?
- You don't ski?
- In the *desert?*

We roll to a stop. Abdul blasts a petite tattoo on the French horn, a door is flung open and all questions are lost in the ensuing clamor. Four young guys in long flowing robes, a couple of them with full turbans, burst through the door like it's home-time at the loony bin. They come running out at us and go bananas on the car. They slap the hood, they pound the roof, they open the doors, they drag us out, they carry us into the building by hands and feet, they throw us onto the floor, they stand over us yodeling some blood-curdling gibberish. They pull out weird honking pipes made from gourds and big flat drums like the ones in Marrakech and they start pounding and honking and walking around us in a circle. I've driven for two hours to be ambushed and eaten alive by overdressed musicians who've been subsisting on the remains of the Swiss tourists whose skis are propped up outside like a trophy.

*   *   *   *   *

- You like the tagine?
- Mmmuuuggmm.
- More tea?
- Mmmuuuggmm..
- Shall we smoke some more kif?
- Mmmm. Yeah. Wow. Guys, that was the best meal I ever had.

Why is it that all men who aren't Anglo-Saxon know how to cook? These four guys, five including Abdul, looked at the pile of vegetables and grains, the chicken, the plastic bag full of little fishes, some lamb sausage and some flat-bread and the bucketful of herbs that we lugged out here, and they all knew exactly what to do. Almost no words were exchanged. There was no apparent rush. We all have tasks allotted by some telepathic triage. I get to roll the joints and shell the peas, and in no time there's a feast. The chicken gets pineapple and raisins, the cous cous gets prunes and dates, the fishes get dill and almonds, the salad gets lemon juice and olives. There's fruit punch and fresh mint tea, there are green figs and black figs and bare hands and juices dripping off our bare elbows. And it's all accomplished like a languorous ballet where the making and the waiting and the eating and the clearing away all seem to have the same emotional value and nobody is in charge. And after the cooking and eating there's the smoking and drinking, the burping and farting, the rugs and the pillows, the whole kif and kaboodle.

Abdul asks for music. He wants the guys to hear the new tapes I've been playing for him while we've been driving across the desert, music I bought in assorted soukhs, here and there, Bluesy Arab girl-groups wailing. I walk out and fire up the pastel poodle patiently sitting outside in the starlight, resting up after a day of automotive melodrama. Every good doggie has his day and this is his. I crank the radio up to eleven and open all the doors and the roof. Music pours out into the night and through the windows of the café at the end of the world.

The boys all start rolling their heads to the sounds, eyes closed on their pillows, off somewhere in that pussy-laden Paradise they've all been promised. The poodle wails and many miles away a lonely little lady Renault falls in love.

The drums have been leaning against the wall up to this point. But with the communal digestion, gravity working its magic, and with the end of the tape and the silence of the poodles, the boys pick them up and start to play. And this time it's not the loud, honking wild welcome that scared the crap out of me. Now it's an aural pillow, a miasma of soft, lulling rhythms that intertwine around each other. It's call-and-response, but each response moves the story forward a little, the music always expanding and weaving. I lie back and sink into my soft featherbed of thankfulness. Soon, they're all sitting around in a circle making music off each other's music. It's exquisite. The top of my head opens like a night-flowering jasmine blossom.

I feel like I've been let into a deep secret. I feel as if the lid has come off the woven basket and the dancing cobra has winked at me. I'm ridiculously happy. I walk wearily up the stone stair and out onto the big flat roof, followed by Abdul the Bountiful. Above us, the huge dune shines away, drawing our eyes upwards to the even bigger blaze overhead. We lie on our backs. There have never been so many stars since the big bang. I wonder if

I may even get a tan. To answer the questions that were left hanging in the air when we arrived, he puts in place the final few tiles that are missing from the mosaic.

What he tells me sends me floating up into the warm night.

He asks me if maybe I know of *The Little Prince?* The Little Prince from the lumpy little planet? Who meets the aviator whose plane falls to earth in the desert? The Little Prince in the book? Yes, that Little Prince. He tells me that this is where the plane crashed. Right here. Here is where it all happened. He explains to me carefully, lest I fail to catch his drift.

Did I step through some rent in the fabric of reality and wake up in a children's story? But then he mentions the movie. He tells me about the film crew that landed here from Paris after flying all around the world, location-scouting. They decided that right here was the only place impossible enough for this impossible story to take place. So here we are then, Abdul and I and the fab four below us and the weary blue doggie asleep outside, all hanging out in the official headquarters of childhood fantasy? Apparently yes.

The café was built for the film. After the movie wrapped the structure remained. These four drummers were movie extras who stayed on, getting food ferried out by friends, snagging the odd tourist like yrs trly and making like the strangest ski-bums ever seriously offered. Ah yes, the skis. The last unanswered question.

I am finally Lawrence of Arabia. Peter O'Toole in a long white frock. I am striding along the crest of a huge white dune as per daydream. There is no warbling of a lone Arabian nightingale, no wispy hint of frankincense. But there *is* the sound of hysterical laughter from Omar and Mahmoun as they ski expertly past us, down the side of the slope, turbans flying, pale-blue djalabis billowing in the moonless starlight, *whoooosh*, for the umpteenth time tonight, slaloming expertly down the impossible piste on their impossible skis, laughing like... well, like stoned Arabs.

I seem to have wandered into the world's favorite book only to find that it is way more fantastical than the published version. I must remember to look carefully in my own copy of it for sand-skiing Berbers, ocean-beds that float above the desert and a café that is not quite possible. I am up here bathed in the light of the Milky Way on whose remote outer edges we are, on our own lumpy little planet. I know from school that the word 'galaxy' comes from the Greek word for milk, and that I'm staring into the center of our own galaxy and that this the best view I have ever had of Home. I can see right through the spilled milk of stars into the white light at the center of the spiral. It all looks… extremely unlikely.

Back in Marrakech, I'm holding a plastic cup of espresso and a return ticket, standing in line at the funky little airport, waiting to fly back to gay Paree, land of the poodle. The circus has left town along with the King and the concubines and now it all feels very different. But from behind me in the line of passengers waiting for the Paris flight, I hear a strangely familiar accent.
- Yo! Moozair fookair!
Well, I'll be *fooked*. It's the Frenchest guy in Morocco. We get on the plane together.
- So. What did you do, Michel?
- Zeece and zat. You?
- Zeece and zat.
When we got back, Paris was warmer, New York was colder, Moroccan memories vaguer. But we had plenty to tell each other, having had two entirely different trips on the same trip, traveling together as only two halfwits could. It was good to hear his funny stories, with the slouch, the shrug, the stubble, the mumble, the shades, the cigarettes, the too-tight pants, and above all, The Accent.
I really miss it these days. He moved to Miami Beach.

ONLY SILK

INDIA

I know a bit about silk. Literally. A bit. As in not much. Wandering around Asia, I've picked up a veneer of expertise. At my age, it's more like a patina. OK, make that a crust.

That lake in Burma where they row with one leg? There's a silk factory on stilts in the middle of it. Been there. Russian Market in Cambodia? Done that. Chewed the fat with silk farmers in Thailand. Even chewed actual silk worms, deep-fried, with the late-night, off-duty bar girls in Bangkok. Oh, the places you'll go! (and the company you'll keep).

But I'm no expert, just a fan. Suffice it to say that when I was in India and showed up at the postcard city of Udaipur, 'Jewel of Rajasthan', I was keeping an eye open for a nice bit of cheap Indian silk.

I was never one for the patterns, the tartans and the other fancifuls. One chunk of raw color looks better to me, and doesn't cost much, either, which is maybe why I always liked the plain colors so much. I couldn't afford anything else. I'd buy them as presents. Then keep them.

So I'm wandering through the back alleys of old Udaipur, eyeing the usual old merch, and in a dark doorway there's a sudden flash of deep purple, a really dark shade between navy blue and a very painful bruise. I stop. I go in and bring the little piece of silk out into the light, followed by the merchant. It's a small scarf, but deep and rich and shiny. Midnight at sea, sort of thing. These very dark colors are a bit unusual in the silk biz, not particularly valuable, just, you know, a bit off the menu.

- You have a good eye, sir.

- Oh, not really.

- But yes indeed. A very, very good eye, sir.

- I'm no expert.

- I disagree. Good taste is its own expertise.

- Now you're just buttering me up.

- On the contrary. I understate. A hundred people have passed this silk today and not one has understood its uniqueness.

- I do like it, I must say. How much is it?

- In fact, I was thinking of keeping it for myself.

- Oh?

- Oh yes. We silk merchants can also be seduced by a piece such as this. Quite rare, you know.

- How much?

- Not much, sir. The weave is nothing special. It's all in the color, you see. But you know that, of course. The balance of the rough warp and the more delicate weft is what creates that sort of liquid effect.

- It *is* a bit like liquid, isn't it?

- Mysterious. Profound. Only silk creates such emotions. Only silk. Wouldn't you say so, sir?

- Me? No.

- We silk merchants can still be moved by our own stuff, you know.

- Oh, I'm sure. So how much?

- How much do you suppose?

- Too much.

- Ah. The desire to possess. The fear that you cannot.

He wrapped it around his wrist and fluttered it about in the light. It shimmered like deep, dark mercury. Wow. Now I *really* wanted it. The thought of having stumbled onto such a piece, in this nowhere of a back alley, was like that dream of finding the old Ferrari in a barn. How high would I go? Fifty bucks? Jeez, I hope he doesn't ask fifty dollars, the bastard, now that he knows I want it. I won't pay that. It's so small. I mean, really just a scarf.

- Actually, I have *just* decided to give it away, sir. To you. Yes. I'm
giving it to you. You deserve it. An eye such as yours, sir. The eye
of an artist. Only silk has poetry such as this. Only silk. So it's yours.
For free. It's a gift. One silk lover to another. Here. Take it.
He draped it over my arm. I was speechless. I started to yammer and
stammer at him to the effect that I could not *possibly* accept such fine
silk as a gift. We waltzed back and forth, I insisting on paying, he slowly
being persuaded to accept a token sum. We settled on $25, although I
was sure it was worth more, even though it really was a *very* small
scarf, I had to admit. *Very* small in fact. But what quality. I damn near
strutted down the street after handing over the equivalent in rupees.
Wow. "Only silk creates such emotions. Only silk." I kept repeating his
words on the flight home. What a score. And what a story to tell.

Back home, I took a long look at it in the bright sunlight of my
yard and yes, it really was as deep and rich as I remembered. No doubt
about it. A rare piece, he'd said. Along the edge there was a small bump
peeping out almost invisibly from the seam. Closer up, with my
glasses on the end of my nose, I could see that there had been a little
tag, but that it had been purposely sewn into the seam, probably done
by the weaver herself, not wanting to disturb the simplicity of the
little scarf she'd just made. In Burma, or Cambodia, for instance,
there is almost never any indication as to who made even the most
amazingly complex pieces. It's a sort of artistic modesty, a desire not
to interfere with the purity and symmetry of the thing. Sort of thing.
Ah, yes. Only silk creates such emotions. Only silk. My god, how
beautiful everything to do with silk really is. But I was curious.

So, very carefully, I ran a razor blade over the few small stitches that
were hiding the little tab. Slowly I teased it out. Gently I unfurled it.
There were words embroidered into it. I put my glasses onto the end
of my nose and read them. They said '100% Polyester'.

AH, THE JUNGLE.

SAO PAOLO

Her name was Selima. Her father was an Indian from the Amazon with a bone through his nose and a tattooed foreskin. She showed me the photo. Her mother was a topless dancer from Harlem who was clearly impressed by that sort of thing.

Selima's hair was long and straight and so black that no light escaped from it. It might even have caused candles to dim when she entered rooms. She was tall and willowy, with a figure like an hourglass with rather more sand in the top. When she moved it *was* a samba, and each one she passed not only went 'aaaahh', several of them also went to confession.

Even here in beauteous Brazil, she stopped traffic. In fact she caused wrecks. I saw one myself. A guy driving alongside us, keeping pace with us and staring with frank worship at her syncopating little buttocks, drove at three miles an hour into the back of a truck that was stopped at a light. She heard the bang but kept walking. Her only reaction was a tiny smile that flickered across her enormously sculpted lips. She had such a voluptuous pout, that you could possibly have stuck her to a tiled surface. How did I wind up walking next to such a vision? Well, as my friend from Arkansas used to say, "Every so often a blind pig *will* find a truffle."

It was at the bar of my hotel in Sao Paolo that I met her. As I was checking in, I was checking her out. The double take I did when I first glimpsed her will probably cause me severe back pain in later life. I walked over to her with no hope whatsoever, but with that 'let none go un-asked' reflex that guarantees some of us a life of perpetual embarrassment. I stood next to her as she perched languidly on her barstool, long legs crossed, gazing blankly through a plate glass window at the swimming pool outside. Standing so close to her, I was so near to actually *vibrating* with excitement, that I wondered if I might appear slightly out of focus.

I pretended to be waiting for the bartender who was off somewhere serving somebody, so that I could steal swift glimpses at random details, a caramelized clavicle, a delicately turned wrist, a cantilevered cheekbone. In order to do something - anything - I opened my mouth to see what might issue, maybe actual words. What did emerge was a sort of strangulated yammering. For some reason, I seemed to be channeling a cornered ferret.

I yacked away pathetically about god knows what, without a flicker of reaction from her or any acknowledgment that she even knew I was standing there, inhaling her. After an eternity, she turned towards me, lifting her head slightly and raising her hooded eyelids wearily over astoundingly large, dark brown eyes, as if raising the curtain on an erotic melodrama, and whispered,

- Hava da fiyah?
- Excuse me?
- Fiyah. (She waved an unlit cigarette as a visual aid).
- Fiyah? Oh! Fire. A light. Yes, I might have one... somewhere...

I patted myself down. So. She hadn't understood a word I'd said. Not one. The quest was, as usual, off to a flying standstill. My Portuguese was non-existent. How would this wind up? With us barking at each other? And, oh sweet negro Jesus, it began to dawn on me, detail by delicate detail, what a heavenly creature she was, with perfect little curvatures here and there that softened her long and elegant skeleton.

She had been carved out of chocolate by a god with love on his mind and time on his hands. But the chocolate, it seemed, would be in my case of the bittersweet variety.

- Fiyah?

- Oh, yeah. I'm sorry, I was..er... drifting...

There were hotel matches in an ashtray. I lit her ultra-long Marlboro Ultra-Light. With her ultra-long Giacometti-like fingers she lifted up the pack to offer me one. I didn't smoke, hadn't for years, so I took one, lit it, and inhaled hungrily. She smiled at me a warm, forgiving sort of smile as if to say, "Look, you poor bastard, I know I'm ridiculously hot so I'm used to this kind of drooling. Go ahead and hyperventilate. It will pass and you'll be fine."

By way of mute reply, I ventured a sheepish little smile of my own, it's general drift being that I was grateful for her indulgence but that she was to pay me no mind, as I was basically harmless and simply talking to her because I knew that as a comparative Quasimodo on the food chain of which she was the Esmeralda, I would never again be this close to the face of God, but that I wouldn't dream of laying so much as a glove on her. I would be perfectly happy just to hump the furniture in her room, and she didn't even have to be in the room at the time.

There was a pause as we both digested this mute exchange. She looked off again into the middle distance, apparently making various decisions. Then she said,

- Rum?

- You'd like some rum?

- Rum nambah?

- Rum and what?

- Rum *nambah.*

- Oh. Room number? My room number? Um. Seventeen oh seven.

She looked away again, gazing evenly and without hurry, leaving me twisting in the breeze of the air-con, not only unschooled in her language, but suddenly unable to utter in my own, either.

Then she turned and looked up at me and smiled a perfectly childlike smile, unleashing a tiny dimple that affected my knees.

- I go now?

- Go? Why must you go?

- I go seventeen oh seven?

- What? You? Go? To my room? Oh. Yes. Yes, *please!*

Well, I'll be darned. A hooker? Good heavens. Very good heavens indeed. No bar talk? No pretending to be interesting? I get to *have* her, just like that? Just by giving her some money? How very fair. Such a marvelous profession, the oldest.

We rode up in the elevator together. Well, I think we did. Maybe we were just beamed up on some sort of force-field powered by the sudden tightening of scrota worldwide. All I recall is that whatever the upward conveyance, once inside it she gave me the biggest, toothiest smile I thought medically possible and clouds parted throughout the length and breadth of Brazil, and I spent the following week walking in sunshine and tipping big.

A hooker. Well, well. I had absolutely no idea I was even *tiptoeing* down that particular primrose path. Who could have guessed in a thousand cocktail hours that this stand-offish, unapproachable creature would soon be...you know. She looked for all the world like some spoiled trophy, waiting for Hubby to take her jewelry shopping on Paolista Avenue. I had only approached her because I had no choice, my religion compelling me to. Who could have guessed that in less than fifteen minutes she would be standing naked on my coffee table, slowly pirouetting her finer points for my delectation, black hair billowing out as she turned and turned, thermonuclear smile lighting up the far corners of the room? Who could have guessed? Not me.

And to my relief, once we'd had a couple of laughs over the totality of our language barrier, Selima positively leaped from that sullen cocoon and butterflied into her loud, raucous, wild-animal *real* self. Far from being the aloof beauty at the bar, she turned out to be an outrageous exhibitionist and knew every word to every song on the music channel, which she turned on immediately. She sang out loud and bounced around with such total bare-assed abandon that within a few minutes there was probably enough estrogen in the room to spread on a cracker.

I won't describe Selima's nakedness because it will just make you sick. Suffice it to say that I just couldn't take my eyes off her for the next several days. She moved in. We were 'holed up' if you'll excuse the expression. On the second day, she jiggled off somewhere and came back with a little bag of weed and a big bag of girl shit. She proceeded to drape animal-print scarves and x-rated undergarments over chairs and lamps and doorknobs until my sober, earth-toned 'junior-suite' looked as if a voodoo priestess had just set up shop in the back of a Victoria's Secret. I was in town on quite serious business as it happened and occasionally I had to leave the hotel to attend such erotic inconveniences as meetings. But I was a big hit in all of them, because what none of my fellow attendees seemed to grasp was that I was now God.

Occasionally she and I went out to stroll round the block for ice cream, fresh air and the odd car wreck. But most of the time we stayed in our room because she had an insatiable craving for music videos, which in the absence of any possible conversation, played constantly on the big screen at the foot of our bed. From time to time she would just spring up with a yelp and dance around the room to a favorite song, as if she had no control over herself at all, none whatever, like a kitten with a ball. See it. Pounce. Just like that. It was the same thing when she first opened the mini-bar. She screamed and tore the wrappers off *all* the chocolate bars all at the same *time* like some crazed hyena. Rip, rip, rip. Munch, munch, munch. Endearing, yes, but slightly unnerving. No inhibitions at all. No second thoughts. No editing. No self-control. No nothing. I had never seen anything quite like it. Sexy, yes, but, you know... scary.

And, of course, you can't lock up a beautiful woman like a prisoner in this day and age no matter how sincere you are, well not indefinitely anyway, and certainly not in a highly public situation like this rather sniffy hotel. And so the day came, or rather the evening did, when with a series of frowns, grunts and pouts, I was given the big hint that Selima wanted to go out, as in Go Out, as in Dinner. Well, what the heck. I could do with a change. So I said OK. I even went so far as to promise her that we would go to a very fancy place, a very swank spot, the current toast of the town in fact. I thought we could get away with it.

My angel skipped giggling into the shower and warbled some Amazonian ditty beneath the dancing waters. When she walked into the bathroom naked, she looked like a sliver of paradise, a shiny black gazelle gamboling across the lawns of an alabaster palace at the far end of a cul de sac of DNA exploration that was closed to mortals. Thirty minutes later, when she strode out of the bathroom, dressed, she looked like a ten-dollar transvestite at a bus stop.

The transformation was horrifying. She was wearing so much make-up that the weight of it seemed to change the shape of her face. Her lovely mahogany mouth was now pale pink. It looked like a slice of Spam on a blackboard. Those gentle sloe eyes were now encrusted with some kind of aquamarine spackling compound that made her look as if someone had just poked her in both eyes with a trowel. Her hair was teased up so high a pygmy might have just woven a tree house and moved in. She tottered around the room on the kind of stilettos that are sold only at the kind of boutiques that also sell dildos. And she was modeling pink vinyl hot pants that may have fitted her when she was about twelve years old, but which were now so tight they merely formed two raised eyebrows over her narrow bare ass. What had happened to the demurely dressed young lady at the bar? Obviously her experience of 'going out' hadn't included the sort of joint we were headed for, one without a mirror ball and a metal detector. We had a reservation at one of the most refined restaurants in Brazil. She would have been thrown out of a McDonald's.

I was beginning to question the rather ambitious nature of my dinner plans.

As diplomatically as I knew how, I steered her back to the bathroom mirror and began what was basically a dry-dock, hull-scraping process. She was nudged back into the shower. Every attempt at Elegance, quote unquote, was gently rejected. No, you can't put sparkles on your cleavage. No, a miniskirt is not supposed to show actual labia. Back and forth we negotiated; earrings, tube-tops, lip glosses, nail polishes, what have you. It took another hour before I had finally persuaded her into slightly less nose-bleed heels, her former minimal make-up, a simple white top (possibly a bit too tight) and black stretch pants (definitely a bit too tight). She did insist, however, on wearing a big silver juju bangle, but that was fine with me. I was beginning to think we might be needing that for divine intervention at some point later.

But I must say, as we headed out onto the street, checking ourselves out in the grandiose lobby mirrors, I had to allow that with her simple outfit she was as close as she was ever going to get to being Grace Kelly - well, Grace Kelly playing a black hooker. And, come to think of it, I don't recall Grace Kelly's ass bouncing around like two hard-boiled eggs in a black handkerchief.

As I watched her sashay across the forecourt towards the taxis and then spin around to smile at me (and at the couple of other guys who had stopped to look at her) I began to have serious doubts about my choice of restaurant. She looked terrific, yes. She looked like a terrific whore.

Ah, what the hell. We are chauffeured away to dinner in the hotel's very swank Mercedes limo, suddenly offered to us free of charge - just like that - by a hotel chauffeur sporting a perfectly frank boner. It is twilight, a purple gloaming, a magical hour in which everything is possible, and she looks positively regal in the back of the black Benz, languidly crossing and re-crossing those long legs, pluming her cigarette smoke out of the window into the warm night as one to the limo born, juju bangle jangling darkly at the darkling shapes above us. We have one of those moon roofs, so we lean back and take in the tops of the wacky skyscrapers lined up along outrageous Paolista Ave., each one more bizarre than the next, a wild sight, an armada of sore thumbs sailing drunkenly through the wine-dark sky with here and there a helipad stuck like a crow's nest on the top, with even at this late hour a chopper or two touching down and taking off again, jet-fueled humming-birds that feed on only the topmost blossoms. It's retro future. It's a movie. It's *Bladerunner.* We cruise by, my honey and I, beneath this strange plantation of aerial lily pads for heavy-metal dragonflies. From the walnut dashboard a little Latin jazz is percolating like coffee candy. We smile at each other. We're very happy. We're very hungry. We're very stoned, the evening's entertainment being sponsored by Selima's grass, of a quality I had previously only read about.

We arrive at the vaunted *boite.* I have cashed in my one owed favor in Sao Paolo to get a table at this fancy eatery, and as we are ushered in by an oleaginous male model, I begin to intuit the fabulosity. This place is so high-toned that only dogs can hear it. I grasp its semiotic effluvia enough to be tempted to bow from the ankles at everyone in the place. I now seriously wonder if maybe I haven't aimed a little high with my rented wife.

But, as I walk past table after white-linen table and notice the Petruses, the Romani-Contis, the Ornelaias, the Sassecaias and the wines of whose provenance I have no clue, and as I clock the Gucci, the Pucci, the Prada and the whole haute enchilada, the vaguely recognized incognitos and all the sartorial entities and non-entities, I can also not help noticing that they are all in various stages of noticing *us*, or rather of noticing *her* to be precise, and no wonder.

Selima walked into that place the way she probably walked into any joint. Big. To her, it was just another door. She may not know much about the social register, but she sure as shit knew how to make an entrance.

Barely inside, the arc of her hip-wiggle suddenly doubled as if by instinct. Her little plum of an ass was soon swinging from side to side so widely that it graduated from pendulum to weapon. I was worried that she might start clearing tables with it. The torque on the thing caused me to linger a few steps behind her, thereby bearing witness to the unfolding ruckus she was causing as she undulated ferociously, following the maitre d' down the perilous path between tables.

Far from being cowed by all the prevailing poshness, she smiled sweetly at everyone she passed, swaying along, and to left and right she met all the gawking stares with little winks, little crinkles of the nose and little waves of the hand. She acted as if everybody knew her and she were magnanimously acknowledging all of them, the little people, her public. At one table, she even stopped and proffered the back of her hand for kissing to an extremely grand old codger who had in no way solicited it, but who took it, perfect gent, and touched his silver moustache to it expertly. His old wife looked astonished. But maybe that was just the plastic surgery.

By the time we arrived at our table, a very central one of enviable journalistic value and of the highest possible visibility - the maitre d' recognizing a priceless *scandale* when he saw one - Selima was positively humming with wattage and smiling broadly at the world in general. She even executed a little pirouette before she sat down, as if making sure that every corner of the establishment got a load of her prehensile posterior before she removed it from general viewing.

The second we sat down the room exhaled. The ecclesiastical silence that had held during her progress up the nave suddenly exploded in a muted clamor of stage-whispered chatter and silverware. It sounded like a flock of pigeons landing on a tin roof and then slowly settling. The sommelier strode up and looked askance at her, having watched her entrance, snobbish in a way that only a recently penniless Italian can be. He plopped his fat wine list on the table - rather rudely, I thought, - but it fell open as luck would have it, on a page of rather recondite Tuscan vintages, in the middle of which I spotted a name that I knew and - more important - knew that I could afford without a mortgage. Greatly relieved, I pointed to it right away. When he saw what I was ordering and ordering without a moment's hesitation, he almost wept openly.

It was the wine from his home village. And nobody had *ever* ordered it, not once, because nobody had heard of it and it wasn't expensive enough to make anybody curious. When he brought it grandiosely to our table, I invited him to sit and share a glass with us, which he did with great affectation and a lot of shirt-cuff business and leg crossing. When he suggested Selima take a trial sip, she demurred, preferring to drink hers with her meal. Instead, she ordered a Pepsi and was inconsolably miffed when it arrived and it turned out to be a Coke. The sommelier, by now smitten, having gotten a closer look at her undeniable hotness, was mortified on her behalf. In high dudgeon and with a loud rat-a-tat of what sounded like medieval Florentine locution - which got the attention of the entire restaurant once again - he angrily dispatched a terrified busboy to the corner store pronto to rectify the situation Pepsi-wise and thereby to obviate further embarrassment within the international community. This caused Selima to sit up a little higher in her chair and flutter her long lashes at nobody in particular. The birds adjacent began to rustle afresh.

We talked about the wine, the sommelier and I, he knowledgeably because it happened to be the triumph of his little region, I sentimentally because I had drunk it so many times during lubricated evenings in a loud wop joint in Manhattan, a place he knew quite well. So we rambled on about our mutual New Yorkage and other variegated mutualities. His name was Mauro and all the time we chatted he stared, with a mounting want of shame, frankly, directly at Selima who was still looking around, smiling and nose-crinkling and waving, playing with her bangle and touching herself here and there while waiting to shove expensive morsels down the inside of that lovely long neck.

Mauro was clearly having the same gaga reaction to her that I had had, and during the proceedings he would occasionally look over to me and grin foolishly for no apparent reason. Clearly, beautiful women came and went here all the time. There were many lovely creatures here tonight. But Selima was something else, the only actual wild animal in the room, a force of nature, childlike, uncontainable, electrifying. He asked her only one question. "Where are you from?" She answered "Belém". "Ah," he said, "the jungle."

The waiter arrived and described, at numbing length, the special draw of the place - a wood-burning oven in which they created Tuscan dishes of such aching authenticity you would think the extra virgin olive oil had been personally pressed by the Extra Virgin herself and that the oven was fueled by chips of the True Cross. But my child-bride was unimpressed. In fact she was starting to look positively glum as the waiter waffled on. The pout started to protrude. But he finally came to the stars of the show, little wafer-thin pizzas the way they make them in some obscure Italian village - you know the song and dance - and as she heard the magic word *pizza,* she whooped out loud, jumped up, clapped her hands together and knocked her chair over. The nearby tables looked over at us, dismayed even further that the arrival of a palpably red-light element had resulted not only in the best table in the place, but the fawning attention of the snootiest sommelier in town, who even now was sitting bolt upright and loudly applauding her raucous enthusiasm for the best thing on the menu.

Mauro left, all smiles. The fabulous appetizer arrived none too soon, two paper-thin pizzas steaming hot from the oven. I seem to recall they were topped with baby mushrooms, embryonic fennel and unborn artichokes. They smelled great and I was starving. I dived straight into mine, not noticing that Selima had not even begun. She had in fact sat up in her chair and put two fingers into her mouth.

Suddenly she reared back and let out an ear-splitting whistle. Deafening. Hellacious. Dogs stopped in their tracks within a mile radius, I guarantee. The busboy froze, not having been subjected to a sound like that since prison, probably. The entire congregation stared at us in mute, gob-smacked horror, their bodies all stuck at the point they had reached pre-whistle. Forks were raised to mouths, wineglasses poised at lips, knives stopped mid-slice. I too was sitting pillar-of-salt-like, stunned by the horrendous report in my ear. The busboy turned, looking very afraid, and gingerly re-approached our table, cowering in front of her with a sickly grimace, visibly afraid of offending her again after his earlier tongue-lashing by Mauro. He managed somehow to ask her what she wanted. She said one word to him and, proud that she knew the word in English and showing off for my benefit, no doubt, she said it in English and she said it very loud indeed. I will go out on a limb here and bet that it was a word that had never before been heard in that restaurant nor has it ever been uttered since, so electrifying was the result. She yelled "Ketchup!"

The adjacent fowl nearly exploded. Ketchup? Did she say *ketchup?* Flutter, flutter, mumble, mumble. The poor lad ran as if howitzered into the kitchen, marginally more afraid of the whistling *puta* than of the reception his request would undoubtedly receive from the chef. One felt for him. One wondered if he would be seen again. Ever. Anywhere. Ketchup? The word was repeated all around us as the fancy fauna began to mutter in earnest. *Ketchup?*

There was a long cinematic pause after the busboy disappeared into the kitchen and the slowly flapping kitchen door continued to slowly flap like the door on a cowboy saloon and we all stared at it, my neighbors and we two. Suddenly it was flung aside by the heaving bulk of a very large man indeed. The room fell silent. Those of us who did not already know him by repute, recognized him from the portrait that stared out from the cover of this month's big Brazilian celebrity mag. Even Selima, a magazine addict, recognized the famed toque in the doorway and, blissfully unaware of her mortal sin, flashed him her biggest smile of the evening. He glared at her. She waved him one of her little waves. He glared at her. She winked at him. He glared at her. She blew him a kiss. He glared at her.

Slowly, as his glare digested her ice-melting desirability, one could clearly observe the warring tides of hatred and lust herring-boning across the famous brow. His head veins began to subside. He was in more than two minds. He was in a tangled vex of emotional conundra. He took one more look at the lovely Philistine, the one who had uttered the word that shall forever live in infamy, and retreated confusedly behind the door, possibly so that he could kick somebody in the privates, in private.

Flutter flutter. Mumble mumble. Again the neighbors exhale and the feathers refluff. Such drama. From the corner of my eye I catch a glimpse of the same poor busboy flying out of a side door. Selima meanwhile checks herself out in a hand mirror, unconscious of the mounting hoo-ha. After a moment, the poor little guy zips back in the door and disappears into the kitchen, to be immediately pushed out again onto his reluctant stage. Elbows everywhere nudge each other as he walks with great trepidation and ceremony towards our table. Held in front of him at arms' length and slightly aloft, as if for the pre-auction viewing of a gilded Fabergé turd, is a small tray and on it an object of enormous curiosity and almost totemic power upon which most eyes are now focused, accompanied by the entire range of human facial expression. Redder than any sore thumb on Paolista Avenue, floating towards us above all the turned heads, and positively throbbing in the glow of its own contextual anomaly, stands a large family-size bright scarlet bottle of Heinz Tomato Ketchup.

I was reminded of the Springtime for Hitler number in *The Producers*, where the whole audience just sits there in silence with its collective mouth wide open in shock. I looked around to see them all staring at us. I was in a Mel Brooks movie. I was center-stage in an extremely fine comedy of manners, starring my oblivious playmate, who even now was loudly slapping the bottom of the big red bottle so loudly that it echoed around the silenced room like an enthusiastic death knell.

By the time she had buried all trace of her Tuscan masterpiece under a lake of vermillion crud, the slapping had been continuous for what felt like an hour, accompanied by no other sound than the grunting of the slim harlot doing it. Conversation was killed stone dead for everyone. Watching her finish her pitiless spreading of the appalling sludge over the entire palimpsest until not a square centimeter of the original was visible, many in the audience seemed to lose their will to eat.

By the time she had cut it into pie segments and begun to chomp it girlishly, piece by offensive piece, smiling around the room triumphantly as if to say, "Now *that's* a pizza!" they were sullenly looking down at their own meals, dishes they had paid a small fortune for, as if they might gag on them. I looked over at my guileless Goth and shook my head in amazement. I could not have been more impressed. Selima had simply killed the restaurant. She had shut it down. It was a rout. A highly refined center of late twentieth century civilization had just been sacked by a lone Vandal. She looked up from her plate and smiled at me with innocent, radiant, ketchup-smudged glee.

The chef had meanwhile returned and had been standing quietly in the kitchen doorway the whole time, watching in mute apoplexy as his *chef d'oeuvre* disappeared beneath a crimson lake of vulgarity. After a while he turned and skulked back to the scullery, possibly headed for an ashram. He was replaced in the doorway by Mauro, and from the pained look on his face, it was clear he had heard The Whistle and been told about The Condiment. How else to account for the fact that he was now looking around the restaurant at any table but ours, despite the fact that Selima was waving her napkin over her head at him like a teenage tranny at a Madonna concert. He made a big show of spotting someone way off at the far end of the restaurant and darted off, as far away from us as was architecturally feasible.

Selima looked puzzled. She had not caught his eye? But, how could that be? I must say I don't know what more she could have done, short of standing on her head and playing a kazoo with her vagina. And she was clearly upset. I had never seen her not happy. This was new territory for me. She stood up and stamped her foot. She actually stamped it and furrowed her brow, just like Shirley Temple. Well, like Shirley Temple playing a black hooker.

I sensed a new trepidation in the air among the audience, a vague understanding that a big plot twist was in the offing. She had effortlessly ruined everyone's dining experience while in a perfectly blissful mood. What horrors was she capable of now that she was *pissed off?*

Diners stared at her, eager to find out where their evening was headed. Me too. We were now, pretty much all of us, entirely in her hands, in thrall. It was theater-in-the-round. Food was forgotten. The usual chitchat?

Out the window. The entire crowd, stalls and balcony was now unabashedly glued to the action taking place in front of it at our table, where the second act was clearly about to kick off.

Our protagonist, having so recently basked in Mauro's undivided attention would now be satisfied with nothing less. So she simply stood up and wiggled off in his direction to get more of it. I should add that she had a dripping slice of pizza in her hand as she teetered daintily between tables, displaying a dancer's deftness but a certain want of couth, I thought. The assembly began to positively *ululate* as she slowly wove among them, munching determinedly, en route to her quarry. I noticed that people in the back actually began to stand to get a better view. These were people from the topmost laminate of the upper crust, you understand, who had by now given up all pretense of tact and were simply determined to get their money's worth, one way or another.

She treed her raccoon in a far corner. She tapped him on the shoulder, and even from where I was sitting I could see him wince. She whispered something in his ear, turned on her high heels and wiggled back towards me, all eyes upon her. She was smiling mysteriously as she walked, finishing her slice and sucking those long, attenuated fingers with that lovely toilet plunger of a mouth. When she reached the table, she remained standing, winked at me and picked up her wineglass and a fork. What could she possibly be up to? Slowly the birds settled again, as if cognizant of the diva's need for silence. Seconds passed, pregnant seconds, seconds that by some inflationary geometry felt like days. Bit by bit, Selima was slowing the world down. How many action-packed months had we been here already, and still not been served the main course?

She raised fork to glass and looked over at Mauro, who was eyeing her as a prisoner might a firing squad. She rapped out a few tinkly taps on her glass as if signaling a champagne toast at a fancy wedding. Then, raising her wine - an exquisite *Brigante* of perfectly balanced tannins, muted floral notes and subtly forward fruit, the pride of Mauro's forefathers - she pointed to it with the forefinger of her left hand, and yelled across the room at Mauro the second of the two English words that will forever leave a small ding in the halo of this digestive cathedral. She shouted "Sugar!"

For a brief second the two of them, Mauro and Selima, appeared to float together above the vacuum of a group gasp. She had sought Mauro's attention. She had got it. There are no words to describe the expression on his face, not even in Italian. The pigeonry suddenly sounded like microwave popcorn going off. "Sugar? She asked for *sugar?* For her *WINE?*" And so on and so forth and mumble, mumble, flutter, flutter.

Mauro appeared to wobble slightly, or was I just starting to get drunk? No, there he went again. He wobbled. Then, like a good Italian soldier, he retreated. He disappeared into the kitchen, but emerged instantly bearing a small silver bowl and the kind of hangdog look usually associated with imminent suicide. He walked, with as much dignity as he could manage, towards our apocalyptic table. He hovered over it uncertainly, like the dreaming actor who finds himself onstage, unsure of his role. I whispered to him out of the corner of my mouth, "Sit down. We're out of our depth." He sat. There was not one eye untrained on us now. It was frank, collective hypnosis. I took the little sugar-bowl from Mauro and handed it to Selima. The unspeakable, the uneatable and the inevitable now all occupied the same point in the space-time continuum.

There were small muffled groans from all sides as she began her pitiless work. To the small clinking sounds of tiny spoonful after tiny spoonful of sugar, she proceeded to fuck her wine just as gleefully as she had just fucked her food and was collaterally fucking her sommelier, who sat with clenched jaw and crossed legs, trying not to look at the fucking going on in front of him.

In fact, he seemed to be exploring a whole new realm of facial expression. He seemed to be going for the kind of ironic *sangfroid* that James Bond might affect while having a leg sawed off.

She finally stopped stirring, apparently sensing that the wine was now fucked to a turn. She lifted the thick red syrup to her mouth, halting for a moment as those lovely lips touched the rim of her wineglass - an attention junkie in the cross-hairs of ecstasy - then slowly, slooowly she let the scarlet slime slither down that long throat with a great closed-eye display of oenophilic rapture. She licked her lips. She waited. Then she uncorked such a loud, drawn-out orgasmic groan that even I had to look down at my napkin. Faking it for an audience, of course, was the most natural thing in the world for Selima, and the smile that accompanied it was so disarming it was angelic. She looked as innocent and delighted as a little girl in her own backyard, declaring her bucketful of mud-pie mix 'just right', after all her little friends had spat, pissed and shat in it.

Bathed in the glow and wanting to prolong it, now helplessly fond of her, I reached over and took the glass from her hand. I raised it to my own lips and tipped it back slowly. It tasted like cheap jam and crawled down my throat like a sugared worm. I put down the glass. She looked at me with a mixture of anticipation and concern. "Is *better*, no?" she asked with Shirley Temple gravity. "Oh, yes, Selima", I said. "Is *much* better' The look she gave me is something I wish I could carry around in my wallet and take out on rainy days.

Things flew by in a bit of a blur after that. For the record, we were not actually thrown out. We were merely handed our check without having asked for it, a devastating bit of waiterly signage. For the record, I was embarrassed, but mostly relieved that we were not dragged out of there by an angry mob and horse-whipped in the street. We had not even made it to the main course.

Back at the hotel, Selima sat on the bed watching music, showered and wet-haired, but I noticed that she was watching without the usual little head bobs and toe taps. In fact she was sitting there perfectly still. I had never seen her still. Something was wrong.

- You OK, Selima? There was a pause.

- *You* know.

- I know what?

- *You* know.

- What?
- I angry.
- Angry?
- I very angry.

My heart sank. So she had been wise to everything all along. Even with her hopelessly limited experience, she did know a thing or two, but just couldn't stop herself because that's who she was. Poor kid. She had just been putting on a bold front to make the best of things, pretending to be oblivious but feeling every dirty look. I felt like getting down on my knees and begging forgiveness. She looked so delicate and young and helpless sitting there at the end of the bed, her chin in her hands.

- You're angry, Selima?
- Yes. I very 'angry. I...*starrrving.*

* * * * *

We lay sprawled next to each other on our big bed, wolfing our big juicy hotel cheeseburgers, watching some boy band with big hair squealing like *castrati*, back in a world we could both understand, happy as clams, me singing along with the English tunes, Selima doing it for the Portuguese, both of us occasionally dipping our fat fries into our fat puddle of Heinz.

Later, as the music played, I went over to the window and stared out at the big city lights all around and below us. I could see her on the bed behind me, reflected in the floor-to-ceiling glass. She was stretched out on her belly, her hair brushed flat, plain and perfect, all the way along her sinuous feline back, the way I had first seen it, as she bobbed her head to the music, sipping her big hotel Pepsi through her big striped straw. I recalled vividly the snooty looks of the diners as we exited the evening's farce beneath the arch of their collectively raised eyebrow. I also remembered the wink of the coat-check girl and the wide grins of the valet parkers, and the cheers of the dishwashers who had come out of the kitchen ceremoniously to wave a fond farewell to the wild child whose anarchic exploits had been relayed to them blow by blow, as they toiled away, elbow-deep in the stinking detritus of haute cuisine. On balance, I rather liked our side of the equation, but decided, for the record, not to try that again.

Across the dark emptiness, on the tops of the tallest towers, red lights winked on and off into the night, inviting and warning, aerial lily-pads for heavy-metal dragonflies. *Bladerunner.* A movie. Roll credits. Fade to black girl.

IRONY TAKES A HOLIDAY

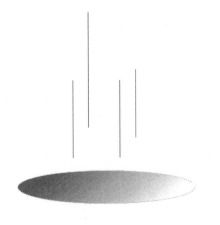

RIO DE JANEIRO

In 1998, friends of mine paid for a holiday in Puerto Rico by helping a guy build his beach bungalow, right on the water. Stumbling along the beach drunk one night, they found a huge bale of marijuana washed up on the sand. Planes often dump these in the shallows near the more remote beaches, and occasionally one goes astray. It's the classic stoner's dream and here they were living it. It was nearly as tall as they were. It was worth an absolute fortune. Broken down into dime bags and sold in New York, where they lived, it would set them both up for years. They were already mentally counting the money and ordering the Porsches.

But they needed to hide it from whoever might come looking for it. So they sawed it into thin slabs and built it into the walls of the bungalow, between the wood exterior and the drywall they were currently installing. Brilliant. Invisible. Nobody could possibly find it.

They went back to New York, congratulating each other and planning to return for the simple retrieval process after the heat had died down. But when they got back to Puerto Rico, there were no slabs of weed in the walls of the beach bungalow. There were no walls. There was no beach bungalow. There was no beach. They hadn't been watching the news. They hadn't heard about Hurricane Georges.

Ironic outcomes have been a feature of my own travels, too. My girlfriend and I once scraped together enough money to go to Rio for Carnival and we had a great time, even joined the parade and danced around with the samba schools along the wide boulevard. Then we got home and watched it on TV and saw the huge grandstands of the Samba-Drome, the big, 100-strong, massed drum bands, the many thousands of spectators. It was stupendous, spectacular, colossal. We didn't recognize any of it. We had flown all the way to Rio and gone to the wrong parade.

OF GOOD FAMILY

THAILAND

There's a joke in Thailand. The hotel manager bangs on your door and yells, "Hey! You got a whore in there?" You yell back "No!" So he opens the door and throws one in.

Having a hooker in Thailand is akin to breathing. Any guy who says that he went to Thailand and didn't 'inhale', so to speak, is probably being sarcastic. So, this is not a story about getting laid in the Land of Smiles. What follows is something else entirely, an occurrence so rare that it may be unique in the annals of the entire region. It is definitely something that sets me apart. Any idiot can get his leg over in old Siam. Only this one can try very hard to, and fail.

It was in Chiang Mai that it happened, or rather that it didn't. Chiang Mai is Thailand's northern city, gateway to the golden triangle, up there where the mountains start and, according to local connoisseurs, home to the most beautiful of women in a country bristling with them. Which is why any man who says he went to Chiang Mai to see the temples is not only being sarcastic, he is also probably standing next to his wife.

I was doing Thailand on the cheap, and if you knew how cheap things were back then, you would have some idea of how broke I was at the time. I walked past the seediest of the seedy guesthouses and took a room in one so unappetizing that I was the *only* guest, which means that it was being spurned on a daily basis by even the most abject of brain-dead hippies. It was owned by a man who rejoiced in the name of Mr. Lightning, but since Mr. Lightning lay around all day smoking opium, occasionally getting up to break into a walk, I assumed that the soubriquet was the work of local ironists.

Oddly enough, I didn't go to Thailand for the girls. Swear to Buddha. This was all before Sex Tourism and there was no Internet yet, so I wasn't, you know, in the know. No, I went there like any other well-educated young man of the era, for the cheap drugs - and possibly because my big sister had dragged me to see *The King And I* at an impressionable age. But once there, the rampant prostitution eclipsed all psychotropic blandishments. I was shocked, I say, shocked.

In certain parts of Bangkok it seemed as if every sentient being was for rent. The most respectable-looking women on the street would smile and say "Hello. I like you. I come your hotel?" Guys driving your tuk-tuk taxi would turn around and say "Hello. I like you. I come your hotel?" After a while, you would half expect the dogs in the street to wink at you and nod in the direction of the nearest alley.

They don't say that anymore, by the way. Now they just ask, "Where you go?" I put it down to a general lowering of standards in the industry. So by the time I ventured north to Chiang Mai, having been in Bangkok for long enough to get the gist, I was well versed in the main component of the gross national product and, deciding to finally take the plunge into commercial loin, being still young and innocent, I got down to business pronto by strolling into the nearest girlie bar, a flimsy affair of wobbly tin and imminent collapse.

It was called *Las Vegus,* the grandiose name grandly misspelled on a rusty tin sign that hung from a big nail outside. Inside, a thin crowd of local ironists was ogling a small stage on which a totally naked girl with a bored expression was opening and closing her labia to the beat of *It's Not Unusual* by Tom Jones. If this mental picture makes you want to rush off to faraway places, I must warn you that foreign travel is not always quite so glamorous.

But as my eyes adjusted to the murk, it began to dawn on me that the wan-looking artiste performing the labial lip-synch was actually rather beautiful. In fact, as she stood up and pirouetted, executing a sweet little curtsey, palms pressed together in that adorable Thai gesture, before putting on her alleged g-string and exiting the stage, I had to admit that she was really quite exquisite, flawless in fact, a porcelain doll of almost ethereal delicacy, by far the prettiest girl I had seen so far in the entire country. A tiny jewel, a little stunner.

I could barely believe that such poetry was allowed into this toilet. As she click-clacked on her tiny stilettos towards the dressing room, I jumped up from my seat and walked up behind her, touched her on her little shoulder and invited her for a little drink. When she said yes and walked back with me to my table, totally naked but for her bit of string, I felt like a teenager who has just asked the prettiest girl in school on a date and, against all hope, she has accepted. She told me her name was Nittiya and that Nittiya means little flower. I resolved, there and then, to take up gardening.

We sat and sipped Mekong Whiskey and Coca Cola, a heady concoction that you can easily replicate by mixing gasoline with jam. When I smiled at her, she would look down bashfully at her tiny hands in her tiny lap. She was busy later that night, she said, tiny voice full of coy regret, doing something "upstairs", but we made a date to meet the following evening in *Las Vegus*, whereupon she would accompany me to my squalid digs and grant me carnal audience. I almost skipped home. I had a date with an angel. I would get to run my fingertips down the small of her small back and say sweet things to her that she would not understand.

The permanently supine Mr. Lightning greeted me from the depths of his personal morphia and invited me to share a beer and a smoke. We lay next to each other on adjoining mattresses of competing filth and inhaled the plumage of his bad opium from a sheet of aluminum foil heated into a trail of smoke by a disposable lighter held underneath. You suck the smoke up a straw - in our case rare antique model, caked in calcified Lightning phlegm. A collector's item. If you were a garbage collector. They call this business with the smoke and the straw 'chasing the tail of the dragon', a rhapsodically romantic phrase for such a sordid task. I was in sordid heaven. Happy the young man who knows he is.

Mr. Lightning wanted to know where I had been and I told him about my little flower. He was horrified. He said that on no account must I consort with denizens of that vile quarter. I assured him that I would be insanely careful and that I was more interested in some sort of petting-zoo vibe than in actually *doing it*, being on the cautious side in that regard. But Mr. Lightning would have none of it and was adamant. He was so outraged that he *almost* sat up. No, no, no, this would not do. He must protect me from myself. I clearly had no idea what I was dealing with. Even if I didn't actually *intend* to do anything with this Nittiya, or whatever she called herself, re the old in-out, did I not know that these girls were *professionally* irresistible? Was I a *total* fool? I didn't answer that question. I wasn't sure of the answer.

Mr. Lightning had a better idea. He would find me a nice girl, a girl Of Good Family, quote unquote, a specie of harlot, yes, but a nice wholesome one, not a full-timer, a gifted amateur sort of thing, more of an entrepreneur, a student type who might simply need a little extra cash for her studies. I protested as forcefully as I knew how, heartbroken at the mere thought of missing the private performance by my gifted little angel. After all, I knew all the words to *It's Not Unusual* by Tom Jones, and tomorrow was my birthday, for crying out loud. It wasn't exactly an expensive gift I'd picked out for myself, but it's the *thought* that counts. I was bereft. But I was also tired. We agreed that I would sleep on it.

At breakfast, Mr. Lightning was a blur of near-activity. From the operational nerve-centre of his mattress, he coordinated plans to make me a birthday cake and throw a party, after which we would sally forth together and comb the town for my choice of the many girls Of Good Family he knew. He was a man with a mission. He had taken a shine to this callow young innocent through the perma-fog of his faculties and wanted to show me how nonesuch were the babes of his burg. I already knew. I was deeply in love with one of them. But protestation was useless and, frankly, would have bordered on the rude at this juncture, so off I ambled into the white morning to rent a motorbike. I intended to putter around the jungly villages surrounding Chiang Mai while he baked the cake and assembled the revelry.

I had no map. But this was when Chiang Mai was still a very small, very ancient place and it had only one ten-storey building on the edge of town, a hotel, from the top of which I could see all I needed to know. To the North was the Golden Triangle, mile upon square mile of scarlet mountainside, carpeted in poppy, fields of waving smack. To the south was the dark river with its shiny tentacles gleaming under the forest canopy, siphoning the fluids of a hundred villages into the wide anaconda that writhed its way down towards the snake-pit of Bangkok and the piratical Gulf of Siam. Aarrh! Jim, lad, that's where I would go today on my birthday, in the hot middle of November, far from home.

This very day in Thailand, I was about to find out, was the day of *Loy Krathong*, a pagan festival of almost criminal beauty, a grand thank-you to the goddess of rain and rivers and streams and puddles. A spectacular thanksgiving by everyone in the land, for the harvest, relying as they have done for so long on the rains for the growing of the rice. The goddess is a river to her people.

Krathongs are little boats made of banana leaves that are set afloat on any available piece of water, to carry prayers to wherever prayers go to. They are launched in flotillas by whole villages onto rivers and streams, or set adrift one at a time by lone farmers on any little pond they can find or just right there in their paddy fields up to their knees in duckshit. Every little banana leaf boat carries incense and flowers, a banknote and a lighted candle. What use the goddess has for cold cash is hard to say, but it is the little flame, or rather the confluence of millions of them, that makes this the day of days and, even more so, the night of nights. So, as I pointed the smoky old Suzuki into the trees, I couldn't wait for the coming dark, when all the little *krathongs* would drift down from the village streams into the River of Kings and transform it into a river of fire, rolling through the center of old Chiang Mai on a cloudless night under the full moon, the river still high from the rains.

As the day wore on in the forest and fields I began to notice many banana leaves with lit candles twinkling on them, floating among the trees, sitting on ponds or sliding by on rivulets, some making their way down to the big river. Villages I drove through were jumping with action. Priests and other pushy characters fussed around big fancy floats as the local beauties were being made-up and buttoned into skintight Siamese costumes, surrounded by hyperventilating boys, and me, because *Loy Krathong* is also the annual beauty pageant, a contest to crown the loveliest of young girls in this world of lovely young girls, the other major crop of Thailand.

They are paraded like toy empresses on thrones in dragon-headed boats, as village vies with village for the honor of having raised the sweetest of the sweet. I was assured that in Chiang Mai tonight, the perfection of these teenage blossoms as they slid by on a serpent of liquid fire would take my breath away. I did not doubt it.

But pretty soon, on a long stretch of red dirt road that cut through the rice fields, my anticipation of the coming darkness was suddenly upstaged by what the daylight had served up as an appetizer. Up ahead of me an old bus was rumbling along under a blistering sun. Normally, I would have zipped around it at the first opportunity, but not this one. This one I would have followed all the way to Burma.

It was full of teenage schoolgirls, all in uniform, and I was suddenly in the throes of the sweetest bike-ride of my young and foolish life. The girls all gathered at the back of the bus to catch a glimpse of this long-haired young *farang* tootling along behind them, smiling like an idiot and waving, stoned out of his mind on good pot and bad opium, wondering what he had done to deserve this windfall of budding estrogen. On that rusty old bike, in a Levi shirt and a sarong pulled up over my knees, round-eyed, and fair-haired and only a few years older than they were, I must have looked pretty exotic to this gaggle of giggling girls in this out-of-the-way place unused, in those days, to the sight of Whitey.

I waved. They waved. I smiled. They smiled. I winked. They winked. They pressed their little faces closer to the glass, beaming. Hmmm, I thought to myself. I wonder how far they'll go with this little Simon Says routine? So I took both hands off the handlebars, pulled open my shirt studs and bared my chest while pulling one of those pouty faces beloved of strippers the world over. The little girls cheered and fell all over each other in a pile of chuckles and nudges. I did a bit of signage to the effect of "now it's your turn." There was a lot of shrieking and shoving and elbowing on the over-crowded backseat, accompanied by blushing and face-covering all around as they nudged and dared each other. I waited, grinning like a chimp, as the big bus went bouncing along.

Slowly, one of the girls - clearly the naughtiest - was pushed to the front of the crowd. She demurely unbuttoned her white school-uniform blouse with downcast eyes and flashed one tiny cup of her little white bra before collapsing on the seat with a lot of feigned embarrassment. I let go both handlebars and pumped my fists in the air. They pumped their fists in the air and the naughty girl got up and took a bow. Then they all pointed to me. My turn.

With some very wobbly riding I managed to yank off my shirt and windmill it around over my head while standing up on the foot-rests and steering with one hand. They cheered. Now it was their turn and now they were clearly feeling a little less inhibited as they all started unbuttoning uniforms and exposing bras, lifting school skirts and flashing their modest white panties, lying on their backs and rolling down their knee-socks and even pushing each other aside to be the next in line to have a shot at their shit-eating audience.

I applauded everything. We blew kisses at each other. They pressed their plump little lips against the window and drew hearts in the steam. And pretty soon it was as if the floodgates of puberty were gently nudged aside as it began to dawn on them that they were all perfectly safe with me, that I was just a harmless young goofball and there would be no price to pay for this sexy little call-and-response panty ping-pong, as the boldest of them flashed their perfectly inflated little white bras. And during all of this they were laughing and waving and winking and blowing kisses and pressing their lips to the window, and I was in heaven, riding behind this girlish, strangely innocent cock-tease as the bus rumbled along. Then, all of a sudden, it stopped dead and I skidded up behind and nearly crashed into it.

We were at a country crossroads, nothing but rice fields and a signpost. A little old lady with a live duck in a wicker basket got off the bus and waddled away, duck-like, down the smaller road. The girls and I were suddenly face to face, only inches from each other. I looked up at them, grinning as before, but not one of them returned my stupid smiles, because I was no longer a distant spectator. I was right there! I was within touching distance. They were totally nonplussed, and had no idea how to behave, with their blouses open and their bras showing and their hair all undone. They looked at each other nervously and then one by one they turned around, pulling their clothes around themselves tightly, silently facing forward, looking either mortified, or genuinely afraid, it was hard to tell. The bus coughed and roared and then moved away and, as it did, I just sat there astride the mud-spattered motorbike in the red road and watched it go, staring at the backs of their lovely heads and their shiny black hair, their topknots, their pigtails, and all their colored ribbons as they drove away into memory and into hours of future fantasy, and that was that. There was nowhere we could go with this little panty-mime. I heeled the bike over and followed the little old lady and her duck down the smaller red road into the forest, full of regret and, by now, stiffer than a Bangkok jail term.

My birthday cake was electric blue, all the way through, and delicious. Mr. Lightning took credit for it, of course, but as he did so from the usual horizontal, I assumed it was his wife I had to thank. The three of us ate, drank and toasted each other many times. Old Lightning and I shared far too many hits of his dubious black tar after which I was plunged into torpid reflection about my birthday, about birthdays in general, about life's aching brevity and one's clueless complicity in it, clinging as we must to the sinking boat we are so poignantly trying to paint. Eventually I was able to stand up. It was pointed out to me kindly that standing up was essential, if we were to stroll out in search of a little icing for the old cake, as it were. So, one last bracing toke on the dragon droppings and we were out the door and into the night.

Now, I don't know what I was expecting, exactly, and my man had been less than forthcoming whenever the subject was broached, but I must say that since our stated objective was female companionship, I found our first stop a tad inexplicable. It was a launderette. Maybe that first twenty yards of near-exertion had tired old Lightning out and he needed a rest? Apparently not. With a lot of salacious nudging and winking, he made it clear that this was our actual destination. The place was empty as far as I could see. Was this all an elaborate front? Or was my future inamorata going round and round in one of those machines? Would she emerge, dizzy but clean, for a quick tumble in the drier?

I gave Mr. L my quizzical look. He responded with an obscene gesture and pointed to the only person in the place, a creature I had not even registered, a rather obese girl in off-white overalls that merged with the faded walls. She was quietly fluffing and folding in a corner, her large back towards us. He walked up to her. Surely this could not be my non-hooking hooker. Visions of the sylph-like Nittiya danced before me as the promised night of labial lip-reading again raised its lovely head and I stifled a sob. I had had a vivid dream about her the previous night. I was the guest of honor at a gigantic political rally in Madison Square Garden and her clever little vagina was up there on a floodlit podium, disembodied, lip-synching to me seductively, breathily, over the huge, hushed crowd, singing, "Happy Birthday, *Mister President....*"

Lightning was standing behind the corpulent employee, addressing a large hairy mole on the back of her neck in a way which seemed far too formal and polite to me in my limited experience of these things. I was waiting for him to squeeze her big bottom or something and get on with it. But he carried on in his quietly earnest way for a good few minutes with no reaction whatsoever from her. Finally he stopped talking, whereupon she stopped folding. Then she turned around and slapped him very hard across the face. He speed-shuffled out into the street and kept on speed-shuffling until I caught up with him and we ducked into a restaurant that had a large tank of tropical fish in the window. I wondered, as one always does in these parts, if they were for show or for dinner.

We were seated, next to the psychedelic fish, by a pretty young thing with a name-tag that was pinned right on the very tip of one pointy breast and read *Pat*. I could barely restrain my instinct to obey, being so horny by this point, thanks to the birds on the bus. Mr. L. ordered a beer and looked sheepish. I asked for a Mekong Whiskey and awaited explanation. 'Pat' patted off into the back. Apparently, according to my new-wave pimp, he had been enquiring in the launderette about the fat girl's thin sister, a very pretty girl he knew via a family connection. He had simply been asking the fat sister whether the thin sister might be in the market for a small student loan. What I had witnessed was the fat sister's uninformed, and painfully brief, opinion on the matter. But I was not to be discouraged by this. The fat sister was probably mistaken about the thin sister, who may well be amenable. His mistake had simply been in speaking to the wrong sister and in not hearing it straight from the whore's mouth, so to speak. I was becoming dizzy. All I could see was Nittiya's little *amuse-bouche* opening and closing to my rendition of *It's Not Unusual*, by Tom Jones, a vision slowly receding into blurry images of garish guppies. Pat the waitress woke me from my reverie with my petroleum on the rocks.

- Very nice, no?, said Mr. L., indicating Pat with his thumb, and displaying a certain absence of couth, I thought.

- Yes, very nice, I said, smiling up at her.

- So how about her?, he asked simply.

Aha! So we were not here by chance, either? The waitress was another of his putative putas? Well, she was a major improvement on the violent laundress, I had to admit.

- You like my friend? he asked her in English, pointing to me. Pat smiled at me awkwardly, blushed, and disappeared again into the back. Lightning rose purposefully from the booth and, tapping his nose conspiratorially, followed her offstage. I had barely taken the first sip of my Mekong when there was a loud commotion in the kitchen and he reappeared, walking backwards and gesticulating to the chef who was brandishing a cleaver.

Back in the street, walking briskly and looking nervously over our shoulders, we regrouped and I suggested we rethink our strategy. This was insane. We could wind up seriously wounded or under arrest. Did he actually *know* any of these girls Of Good Family, or was he just hitting on *strangers* Of Good Family? I pointed out that the city was awash in estrogen of the highest octane, and *on the hoof*. I had only to stand on a corner looking solvent and I would be fought over by a perfumed mob. I must have made my point, because he stopped shuffling right there, threw up his hands and said OK. If I was intent on being so impatient and had no stomach for the more sinuous approach, he would take me directly to a whorehouse. Excellent, I said. But, he insisted, not to that hellacious declivity *Las Vegus*. Fine, I said. Very well, he said, in that case he would personally escort me to the most fabulated establishment in Chiang Mai, nay, in the entire kingdom, a legendary destination among the cognoscenti, a veritable showplace of the vaginal arts. Lead on, I said.

We left the lit sidewalks and plunged along dark, overgrown paths, took short cuts through temples and finally emerged in front of something rather unexpectedly grand. It was what remained of an old colonial garden fringed by tall slender coconut palms, a dilapidated enclosure to what must have been a residence of no small splendor in the days of flaunted wealth. A high wall of fat bamboo had been grown, to keep prying eyes from the big mansion whose grandiose roof was just visible above it. I turned to Mr. L with a look that said Wow. He returned me a look that said I told you so, and stood up a little straighter as he sauntered grandly up to the huge thatched gate and pulled on a long cord, at the other end of which was presumably a distant bell. It was distant enough that we couldn't hear it, but in short order there was a shuffling of feet behind the bamboo rampart, a grunting and a scraping, and the big double gate swung open to reveal a large compound that looked like a grand but bankrupt road-company version of *The King And I*. Well, well, I thought.

We were waved in by the fragile old gatekeeper who left us under a dark mango tree, to shelter from the warm rain that had begun to drizzle. He skittered away across the unkempt yard towards the sprawling two-storey villa that looked faintly Chinese. Around its entire upper floor there was a long cantilevered balcony with carved pillars, sheltered from the rain by the curving eaves of the great roof. The whole place was in an advanced state of rot that did nothing to diminish its ghostly patina of former nobility. Paper lanterns within, in various pastel shades suggested many rooms on its upper floor and added to the aura of the old China trade. If a movie director were looking for a location that said down-at-heel warlord's opium den, this was it. The frail little manikin made it haltingly up the long stairway and disappeared around the corner of the balcony. We listened to the rain and waited. I half expected a mandarin empress in moth-eaten slippers to appear. I was not entirely disappointed.

What did walk out onto the balcony was a tiny old woman with her white hair pulled up into a tight bun. She held herself very erect and stood with long red nails curved over the carved rail. She was dressed from head to toe in spectacular crimson silk - one of those skin-tight Chinese dresses that go all the down way to the floor and up to the chin. It was as if a bright blossom had erupted in a dark castle wall.

She placed spectacles on her little nose and looked down at us huddled under the dripping tree. Mr. Lightning nodded in her direction and made a big show of removing his hat. She looked at him for a moment, then at me, expressionless. Then she turned her back to us and clapped her hands together sharply. A covey of little bats fluttered out from under the eaves. She held one palm out towards us as a sign that we should stay where we were. We stayed where we were.

And then slowly, in response to her signal, a vision appeared. Tiptoeing around the corner, in the same regal dress but this one in palest lilac, a slim young beauty with her shiny black hair cut into long Chinese bangs, teetered daintily from one end of the balcony to the other on high wooden sandals that clattered, her little steps restricted by the severe tightness of the long silk sheath. When she reached the far end, she stopped, looked down at us and us gave us a little bow. My heart pounded, perhaps audibly.

The little old lady in red made the merest of gestures with her tiny wrist and around the same corner came another girl, equally beautiful, identically shod and dressed, but this time all in silver silk. She wiggled along in the same shuffling clip-clop as the lilac girl had, and stood at the far end of the balcony next to her. They giggled at each other and the silver girl bowed to us shyly. Then around the corner came a girl in emerald, then a girl in gold, then one in pink, then one in ice blue, one in purple, one in scarlet, one in turquoise, one in yellow and thereafter in every other shade of the silk rainbow until there were about thirteen or fourteen of these almost impossibly lovely creatures standing next to each other, waving and giggling in a willowy chorus-line of pretty maids all in a row. Mr. Lightning let out a long, low moan and said something to himself in Thai. I think it meant Holy shit.

The little red mama-san turned towards us and, slowly sweeping her arm in a grand gesture that took in the entire chorus line, smiled a smile that said *Ta-dah!* She gestured for me to approach the building. I stepped slowly and reverently towards the long stairway as another might approach the altar of St. Peter's. I lifted up mine eyes unto the angel choir peering over the balustrade looking down at me to see what their prayers had brought them, or possibly to see what the cat had dragged in. I was actually feeling a bit bashful at the prospect of meeting this naughty string of pearls. I also had another niggling thought. I wasn't at all sure that I could afford such fancy morsels. I felt entirely out of my depth, truth be told. But screw it. I had to play this hand out as far as I could. I would wing it on bullshit and wangle it on charm. I just wanted to wander a while through the parlors and boudoirs of this aromatic and threadbare pavilion, this ode to Orientalist nostalgia, arm in arm with a silken vision or two before they found out that I was *not* the eccentric millionaire disguised as a backpacker, but a sexual mendicant, a charity case, a bum's rush back onto the street. As it happened, I need not have worried.

As I put my foot on the first blessed step on this stairway to heaven, all hell broke loose. A squeal of brakes outside the high wall stopped everyone dead. There was a clatter of boots on metal, the honking of a big truck horn and a bang bang bang on the gate which sounded close to being brought down by whatever maniacs were on the other side of it, hollering to get in. Everyone on our side of the fence froze. Then we all shouted at once. Little red mama-san screamed at the girls. The girls all clattered back along the balcony and disappeared, hue by hue, back around the corner. The old man yelled some question at mama-san who yelled some instruction back at him while she descended the stair, which in turn sent him running into the house, yelling at somebody else. I yelled at Lightning. Lightning yelled at me. Both of us wanted to know what the *McFuck* was going on here.

The guys outside the gate were yelling through the fence at us to let them in. Well, I guess that's what they were yelling. I started to stumble around, looking for some way we could slip out the back of this joint, but Little Red yelled at us to stand still and do nothing. Then she yelled at the house in general and a naked man shot out from the basement with some strange flapping rag on his ass. Was he a client? I don't know. But if he was, he was sure getting his money's worth. He ran at the gate and threw the big bolt, whereupon the huge doors crashed inwards and a big green army truck full of soldiers, all with Kalashnikovs at the ready, roared into the yard, skidded to a stop and disgorged its platoon, who formed a big circle around all of us, mama-san, the naked man, Mr. Lightning, and me, pointing their weapons not at her, not at them, only at me.

There was silence. The rain fell. The night birds sang. The crickets cricked. Nobody moved. I nearly shat.

Into the circle strolled the officer in charge, a greasy, murderous-looking little twerp with some kind of ascot tied raffishly round his throat and one of those weird little batons of authority jammed under his armpit. I've always wondered what they are for. For delicately lifting toilet seats? For magic tricks? Anal probes? He lit a cigarette with great theatrical panache, stick under armpit and, looking me up and down with a sardonic smirk that he no doubt practiced in front of mirrors, said something suave to the troops who laughed as required and lowered their weapons. I exhaled.

He then said something equally urbane to Little Red and she gave him the same kind of fawning chuckle. He was quite the lounge act. He stood in front of me and smiled, clearly winding up to another drollery, but just as he was about to deliver the zinger, there was a shout from the house, where the little old man was waving a small paper package over his head. The officer turned and beckoned him with his little wand. The old man struggled over to the officer and handed him the package. The officer hefted it in his palm as if weighing it. He then slid it directly into his tunic without opening it. He inclined his head towards mama-san wordlessly. She gave him an equally subtle bow, equally mum. He barked an order to the platoon and they clambered back onto the truck, which he then mounted, standing roguishly on the running-board as it backed out, turned and disappeared. The bare-assed punter ran after them and began to close the gate. Mama-san said something to Mr. L and then, together with the old man, climbed wearily back up the long stair. Lightning tugged at my shirt and hustled me out of there as the big gate was closing, with me still wondering what I had just witnessed and my heart still going fifteen to the dozen.

As we lurched along in the dark and the rain, he wised me up. According to Lightning it had been our spectacularly foul luck to alight upon cloud nine at the precise moment that the local colonel chose to pick up his occasional payoff. The sabre-rattling was to remind Mama-San exactly with whom it was she was dealing and with whom never to fuck; the Army, Pussy-Tax Division. We shambled along glumly towards the Lightning rent-a-sty, hit the mattresses, smoked a little more of his stool sample and bemoaned the ways of the third world as he ran down the litany of local graft. It was a long list and, according to Lightning, involved everyone, from the government to the drunken dwarf who ran the local toilet-unblocking cartel. I was shocked, I say, shocked.

Then, suitably sedated and the rain having abated, I wandered back into the night to see what further fiascos it might hold in the realm of unrequited love. This was after all, still my birthday and by now I was hornier than a bag of antlers. The beauty queens in the villages. The girls on the bus. The angels on the balustrade. Pat the serving wench. Nittiya the labial linguist. Sweet tumescent Jesus. The kettle couldn't take much more steam. But halfway along the street, a glimpse of a lighted candle drifting by on a dark canal reminded me that it was still the fabulous night of *Loy Krathong,* that I still had money in my pocket and still knew where to find the hands-down winner of my own personal beauty pageant. I picked up the pace in the direction of the river, the old *joie de vivre* seeping back as usual. I weaved through the heaving mob in the packed center of town until I elbowed my way to a good view of what all the fuss was about. I had been told to expect a miracle. I was not disappointed. I won't make a meal of this since, story-wise, it's only a snack. But this was something else.

The big river runs right through Chiang Mai, outside the old city wall, broad and high-walled, with a road running along its embankment and several bridges spanning it. All of the above were mobbed with gawkers. The entire river, turgid and muddy by day, was aflame, a carpet of white fire from bank to bank and for as far as you could see, thousands of candle-lit *krathongs* sliding by slowly like twinkling white lava. And sailing upon it were all these illuminated floats of wild Siamese design, being maneuvered to and fro, the better to display the charms of their charges, little teenage orchids on their shiny thrones, smiling and waving at the crowd, all of whom were hooting and hollering for their baby-doll of choice. I found myself looking away and then looking back again just to make sure that the mind was not exaggerating what the eyes could barely credit, that I was actually there and a part of it.

Ah paganism! - the last hope of the crowded earth. Why is it that the more gods people have the happier they look? Next to this kind of sexy jamboree, that One God looks like the dreary old spoil-sport *she* really is. Oh, they're all officially Buddhist here, of course, but not tonight. Tonight's wild, drunken thank-you for the rain *to* the rain is pure instinct. And it's cool to have a goddess of rain, a specific chick to thank, don't you think? The more gods the merrier. Life is just a big party for the blind, anyway. B.Y.O.G. Bring your own god. Different venue, same delusion, same bowl of cherries. Rock on.

Of course, I wasn't thinking about any of this at the time, you understand. No, throughout the entire extravaganza, the flotilla of fire, the armada of arm candy - all no doubt girls Of Good Family - I had only one thing on my mind. So, with a head full of spectacle, I fought my way out of the mob and back to the big front door of *Las Vegus* with a spring in my step and song in my heart; *It's Not Unusual*, by Tom Jones. Screw old Lightning, the rancid old fart. What did he know, anyway? And for that matter, screw the first rosy fingers of dawn over the Taj Mahal and the sunset over the frigging pyramids. I knew real beauty when I saw it, of Good Family or of Not, and here I was on the verge of seeing it again and this time covering it with kisses and running my fingertips up and down the small of its small back. I stood there on the threshold for a long, delicious moment, savoring my anticipation and marshaling my opiated wits in preparation for the long-awaited and oft-postponed ascent into my own personal heaven. It was a long, delicious moment that I should not have taken.

SCREECH! SLAM! CLOMP! CLOMP! CLOMP! I spun around. What? Oh, no. You're kidding me! Not again! I couldn't believe my eyes. It was *them* again, the poon platoon, guns drawn, jumping down off that same big army truck and forming that same circle around me, pointing their same heathen blunderbusses at me again and grinning, actually grinning. Are you motherfuckers *serious?* What could I possibly have done now? Well, whatever it was, I was clearly in deeper shit than before, because I must have been under surveillance the entire intervening time. But why me? All I had done was toke on some tiny turds of bad opium. But what could I possibly say in my own defense? That I didn't inhale?

Into the circle stepped the same military fop with the same faggy ascot, the same silly stick and the same arched eyebrow. He stood right in front of me, arms akimbo, and asked me loudly, to a chorus of fawning giggles from the ranks, "OK, you! So! Where you go?"

Where I go? Where I *go?* I had one hand on the doorknob of a whorehouse. Where you *think* I frigging go? Disneyland? I looked back at the officer and, for some reason that I can only put down to an occasional suicidal tendency, smiled and said, "Me? I go in here. Why? Where *you* go, baby?" There was a long dramatic pause. Then he blurted out "Where *I* go, baybee?" mocking me, ham that he was, and looking around at his back-up singers for full effect. "Where *I* go, baybee?" he said again. Then he shot out his arm and pointed his extended finger skywards, directly over my head, as if – I swear to God – as if about to shout, "Shoot him!" But instead, his face suddenly gashed open into a wide toothy grin, unfurling an acreage of ivory that only Asians seem to own, and he declared with great glee, "I go *up there,* baybee! I go *upstairs* for facking, baybee! Facking upstairs is *number one!"* Then he let out a blood-curdling roar of laughter, stepped around me and, still tittering to himself, disappeared into the dim bowels of *Las Vegus*. The squaddies broke rank and followed him in, guns, ammo and all. One of them even slapped me on the back as he went by. They were all pumping their fists in the air and chanting "Facking nambah wan! Facking nambah wan! Facking nambah wan!"

Ah. I see. Yes. So that's what my little lotus blossom was doing 'upstairs' last night. Well, what did I think she was doing? Knitting? But that didn't make it any less nauseating for me to picture my alabaster cherub being gang-banged by half the army, all standing to attention, no doubt. And to think that two minutes earlier she was all mine if only I had just plunged straight in. Typical. Dithering twerp. Hamlet, without the poetry.

I stood there for a long time, staring down at my muddy flip-flops, savoring the dimensions of my disappointment like a dog worrying a meatless bone, picturing my delicate little virtuoso renting out her musical instrument at fifteen minutes per duet to that conga line of armed comedy. Not a harmonious vision. For the merest moment I considered the possibility that she may be up there remembering our date and demurely refusing them all, waiting for me instead. But a gale of filthy laughter from the upper room, followed by shrieks of girly giggling pretty much laid that one to rest.

Should I stay or should I go? Was I blowing a private audience? Or was she blowing a private? The odds were on the latter. The problem was not that I wanted some exotic sexual adventure, but that I wanted *her*. Here in this gutter of carnal commerce, with the rain pinging loudly off that tin sign swinging from its rusty nail, I had fallen like a ton of bricks, like a schoolboy, for a little bone-china ballerina, a fey twirling figurine that belonged on top of a belle-epoch music-box, but was currently upstairs under a heap of military hog-sweat, being reamed rigid.

The raindrops got bigger and started to run down the back of my bent, hang-dog neck, so I turned away and skulked off into the dark with all the swagger of an empty wind-sock, like a spare prick at a wedding. Brilliant. Couldn't get laid in a whorehouse.

I wandered off, following the rainy embankment downriver until outside of town I came to a big stone weir built across the water to slow the flow. Under the rim of it, as the flaming river rolled over, scores of little boys were catching the *krathongs* as they came flying over, snatching at the little banknotes like gannets and stuffing them into big plastic garbage bags, laughing and yelling at each other and passing cans of beer among themselves in a most un-spiritual fashion, cheeky little bastards.

Another silk veil lifted. Well, where did I *suppose* all that cash went to? The Goddess? Did I have *no* grasp of the real world? And while we're on the subject, did I seriously expect a top-flight *Las Vegus* performer, privy to major military maneuvers, like the daring raid that very night on a heavily fortified compound, did I expect her to forgo all that civic responsibility, just to accommodate the callow yearnings of some stoned white boy who actually admitted to knowing all the words to the lamest frigging song ever seriously offered? Was I a *total* fool?

That question again.

Next morning I took a bus back to Bangkok with the sun coming up and the correct answer to it also finally dawning on me.

BITCH MAGNET

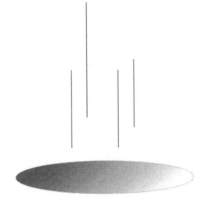

HONOLULU

My old black Volvo was a weird little lump of ironmongery, but I loved it. It was a '59, the model with a rear end that swoops in one long curve from the roof right down to the back bumper. It was meant to look sleek and aerodynamic. But in black, as mine was, it looked like a shoe for a very large clubfoot.

It was way out of style and way out of place in Los Angeles back then in the late 70s, when most American cars had *hoods* that were longer than this entire vehicular stump. But it did have one thing going for it not listed in the manual. It had a pulling power that had nothing to do with the engine, if you catch my drift. I had a brief 'thing' with the cute girl I bought it from and an another brief 'thing' with the even cuter girl I sold it to, and between those two automotive highlights, I enjoyed a level of traction that was unique in my motoring experience.

You hear about these 'performance' cars, but you don't really believe they exist until you see one in action. That little Volvo was the genuine article. There was a vibration coming off it before you even turned the key. It made you believe in things like harmonic convergences and those rips in the fabric of reality where you step into a different dimension, a dimension of… well, of *pussy,* basically.

And you'd never think so to look at it. A few surfers drove old '59s. They would knock out the little rear window and cruise around Malibu with their boards sticking out of it like a middle finger, so it had that tiny thing going for it, but otherwise it was a little runt and I bought it only because I couldn't afford anything cooler.

My previous car had been a real ride, a dream car, a shark-blue classic '64 Cadillac de Ville, all fin and chrome, slicker than snot on a doorknob, but attached, unfortunately, to the girl in Hollywood that it came with, and who had just left me. Technically, it was *I* who left *her*, but since she'd unplugged a heavy desk telephone and thrown it at me as I ran off her property, yelping, the point was moot. She kept the Caddy.

So for the first week or two of my being crammed into this little ugly duckling, after swanning around the City of Angels in such grandeur, I skulked around like Quasimodo and took a lot of back roads, hoping nobody saw me in this goofy little black can. But then I began to notice that women just went gaga over the thing whenever I parked it. It was European. It was different. It was cute. Who knew exactly what it was? It was *possessed*.

And it didn't take me long to figure this out, either. It picked up its first girl for me in a matter of days, and she was a total stunner, a tall blonde from Texas, not usually my type, but only because I couldn't usually get *near* that type. And I wasn't even *in* the car when it pulled her into its web. I was just standing next to the thing. To be precise, I was slowly falling down the side of it.

We both were, my friend and I, falling against it and howling like dogs. We were practically crying with laughter at a story he was telling me about catching his cock in his zipper in the middle of a Vegas show that starred some famously sappy crooner, I forget his name.

The thing is that it was a real fancy ringside table he was sitting at, with his girlfriend and another couple. And they'd been watching the show very sedately, sipping their champagne and so on. This headliner had even been occasionally leaning over and singing personally to the table, the way they do.

He was a really big name. Old school. You know, french cuffs, hair lacquer, sincerity, the full nine. I wish I could remember his name because he was such a famously smarmy bastard that it makes the story all that much funnier if you can picture him with the silk handkerchief and the bullshit. Anyway, the girlfriend, halfway in the bag at this point, decides to slide under the table when nobody is looking and unzip my friend's pants. So when this famous lounge act comes back to the edge of the stage to serenade the table again, there are now only three people sitting at it. For some reason, he starts crooning directly at my friend, singing one of those deeply moving you-light-up-my-life sort of deals. And my friend *is* deeply moved. He's getting a blowjob.

He's just staring glassy-eyed at this syrupy household name, because things are coming to critical mass under there, if you catch my drift. But the singer won't go away. He's found somebody who looks like he's really transported by the song, just staring at him, his facial expression getting more bugged out every second. The guy leans right over him and for a second they're glaring right into each other's eyes, and by fabulous coincidence the crooner comes to his big finish just as my friend does, squeezing his eyes shut, going red in the face, throwing his head back and letting out a stifled moan like a dying coyote, or to be more precise, like a guy who's coming in his girlfriend's mouth in front of a roomful of obese slot addicts.

The singer? Ecstatic. Never had such a reaction. Never went over so big. He's thinking World Tour at this point, especially when my friend picks up a napkin and starts wiping *real tears* from his eyes. The singer takes a huge bow and walks away, strutting like Tom Jones on a victory lap. He probably doesn't bother to wonder why, the next time he looks at the table, there are once again four people sitting at it and they're laughing like hyenas.

Anyway, the band kicks off the next number. My pal, somewhat recovered from his musical experience, reaches down under the tablecloth, suave as you please, and delicately tries to zip up.

But the inflatable is still a bit too XXL. So he gives a good solid yank at the machinery to force it over the hump, so to speak, and *Wham!* - the zipper digs its teeth deep into the actual meat at the tip of the hotdog! *GAAAAAARRRRGGGGHHH!!!*

He screams at the top of his lungs. Bounds to his feet. Over goes the table, the food, the champagne, everything. Blood everywhere. The place goes nuts. Women screaming. One old girl faints dead away at the next table. Mayhem. Everybody yelling. Imagine the carnage. And did I mention *he's wearing a white suit?* Great detail. They carry him out of there, hemorrhaging and honking, to rush him to the E.R. for a transfusion. Band? Silent. Show? Over. People are still screaming, and the last glimpse my friend has of the singer is of him standing there with the mike in his hand and this weird look of awe on his face like 'Holy shit! I'm *that good?*'

So the way he told it, we're doubled over against the car, honking like geese, totally uncool, as this stunner strides up. But instead of giving us a wide berth like the rest of the pedestrians, she stops and stands right over us in her high stilettos and super-short skirt and - *hmmmm, glimpse of white thong* - and she's looking down at us, not like you'd examine something in a Petri dish, but with a big smile. She wants to know what's so funny. And is this your car? Why, it's just so cute. And what kind is it, anyway? Swedish? You don't say! Yes I'd *love* a little drive in it. You can drop me off at my place if you like. It's just up there in Laurel Canyon. And is this a joint in the ashtray? Oh my! And can we smoke it right now? And is that an English accent or are you just gay?

That's the kind of machine this was, the Volvo, or *The Vulva*, as I took to calling it. For so toothsome a creature to just walk over and pick me up like that, she would normally have to be under professional hypnosis. And she even turned out to be a terrific girl, too, as well as a top-shelf pole-dancer. Oh yeah, a featured stripper at the fabulous Kit Kat club, no less. She also had the first implants that I had ever been allowed to *actually touch*. I was mesmerized by them and spent many happy hours just lying in bed marveling at the darn things while she slept on her back. Well, she had to. They made me think of Philippe Petit, that French guy who once walked a high wire between the twin towers of The World Trade Center in New York when they were still standing. As she lay there, I used to stare at those two high-rises and imagine making a fortune by training a flea to hold a tiny balancing pole and walk back and forth on a thread between her nipples. I was convinced it would make me enough dough to set me up in New Orleans.

New Orleans was my big plan at the time, my next brilliant move. I was besotted by the very thought of it - the music, the Mississippi, the voodoo, the cholesterol - and I talked about little else for a long time, but I needed more cash to swing it. So I made a fateful decision. After nearly a year of non-stop, top-notch, pick-ups, thanks to *The Vulva*, and after a lot of soul searching, I sold the magic '59 to the latest female car enthusiast who had strayed into its force field. It was a painful decision. The car had been my free pass to an unprecedented run of luck in the realm of estrogen. I had been practically caked in it from the minute I got behind the wheel. We had been an unstoppable combo, me and the 'V'-hicle, and yet here I was walking away from my partner for a few measly bucks. I felt sick about it, but I was even sicker of LA and needed the money pronto to get out and could think of no other way. So, with my filthy lucre in my shameful pocket, I dragged my ungrateful ass to buy the airline ticket to start my destiny-ordained new life in New Orleans. But the travel agent, *aggressively* gay and with major-league attitude, said, "Noo *Awlins?* Why the fuck do you want to go to *that* sweaty shit-hole? You can get a ticket to Hawaii for the same price."

So I did.

And my fears seemed to be unfounded re walking away from The Magic Bus. The run of luck just continued. My car had apparently forgiven me. In fact, it seemed to have given me the old thumbs up, patted me on the back and wished me all the best, because it turned out that my cantilevered Texan had lived in Hawaii herself and had a girlfriend who was still there and she called her to introduce me. They had been strippers together at the same club. This was her parting gift. She was a total doll, as I said. And when I showed up in Honolulu and met the girlfriend I could hardly believe my eyes. She was astoundingly beautiful, a slim brunette, lissome and tan, with long, straight hair, one of those walking heart-attacks you see on the beach, nearly naked in an alleged bikini, looking flawless and bored, standing next to some big slab of meat with murder in his eyes. She was way out of my league.

But she gave me the benefit of the doubt, thanks to the introduction, which was itself thanks to the car, which was clearly still casting its benign spell. That first night, she drove me to her place up on Pukalani Heights, a very swell neighborhood indeed, high up on the bluff where the couth of Honolulu look down on the uncouth of Waikiki. It was a dream home, a glass box on the edge of the drop-off, heavy with the scent of night jasmine and money. Both she and her surroundings had that same languid air I have always associated with the absence of an overdraft. I imagined she belonged to some blue-blood local family. And later that same fragrant evening, I was in the throes of a very upscale encounter, inserting myself into the ruling class, so to speak, coming into money, as it were, when at one point during the proceedings, she said something that sounded a tad over-privileged, not to say spoiled-brattish - I can't remember what it was - so I seized upon this opportunity to put her elegant, thoroughbred limbs over my knee and affectionately spank her perfect little bare bottom. It was intended as a moment of levity, a love-tap that was supposed to say, 'Oh you naughty little rich girl' sort of thing, and make her giggle and squirm and cover me with kisses. But somehow, in my enthusiasm, I must have very badly miscalculated on the old back-swing and follow-through.

In a word, I *over*-whacked. It was a terrible miscue, a sickening *THWAK!* It rang out like a rifle report that echoed through the quiet, nocturnal canyon so loudly that bats probably flew into tree trunks, and was followed by an appalling silence. I looked down in horror at her round little rump and it's livid, glowing hand-print. What a chump. I could see myself making the Walk of Shame back down the hill. So much for The Great Lover. I had just fucked *myself.*

Finally she spoke, very quietly, almost to herself. She said, "I see." I waited for the other high-heel to drop, something along the lines of "I think you should go now." Instead, she said, "What sign are you?" I told her my stupid sign and nothing happened for a few moments. Then she started slowly to raise her tiny bottom off the bed, elevating that narrow, perfectly inflated little plum in a slow, upward curve, with its bright red rebuke throbbing into the night. Little by little, she continued to raise it heavenward, as one might a sacrament, arching it into the air until it stuck there, glowing in the dark, like a beacon for sex-crazed moths. Apparently, Scorpio was the right answer.

I moved in. And it was the start of a dream interlude for me. I worked on my tan and on my new girlfriend. We would loll around all day and get loaded on her fiendishly powerful pot, and every so often she would drive down the hill into Waikiki for half an hour or so, come back with a carload of groceries and wouldn't let me pay for a thing. My duties were basically to service her as much as I could without having an actual hernia and to whack her on the ass whenever the conversation lagged. I was also required to tie her up from time to time, slap her around a bit and to not listen to her if she said Stop! or Enough! or You Brute! or any other cute little yelps in that same girly vein. I learned the parameters of my servitude in no time at all and cannot remember ever having been so intellectually fulfilled by the convoluted sexual conundra that bound us. I had been hired to be her boss.

As for me, I was working for food and she was it. We had answered each other's prayers, basically. So I would just loaf around alternately caressing her and working her over. It was a marvelous occupation, like kneading clay that had a pulse, sculpting a perfect relationship.

I was the pig in Pygmalion. She was the gal in Galatea.

We knew nothing about each other and she wanted it that way. There were things I was dying to ask her, but I was too busy running my hands over every lilt and curve, every supple subtlety. Who was she? I had no idea. But, as Buddha once said when asked if there is a Supreme Being, 'It is none of our business.' I was merely following the orders I was ordered to issue. For week after warm week, I was her salaried Svengali, her devoted de Sade. I was enraptured. I wanted this to go on forever. And it seemed as if it might, right up until the day she decided to do something that didn't involve, you know, the usual.

One day she decided that we would go sailing. So, on a blue Pacific afternoon, she and I found ourselves strolling barefoot along the privileged planks of Honolulu's most private yacht club, past a bobbing chorus-line of shiny behemoths, the type of expensive pond scum that is owned by the other type of expensive pond scum. We meandered along hand in hand until we arrived at the one truly lovely vessel in the entire marina.

She was a dream on water, a very long and slender sloop with a woman's name and one fabulously tall mast, a wooden ocean racer built in the 30s and maintained in the same ship shape as the day she first slid her prow into the deep blue. She was all teak and brass and curve. There was not a straight line on her. But there were a lot of sunburned men on her who clearly had not been straight for weeks, thanks to liberal rations of whatever cocktails are preferred by mariners of means. The oldest among them, a graying playboy who would have been played by George Clooney in the movie, noticed us and bounded over to help us aboard with a lot of hugging and kissing of my bronzed dream-girl. All the guys seemed to know her rather well, in fact, and were all clearly very pleased she'd shown up, even with another guy in tow. In fact, they were all so exceptionally nice to me that I felt I was being welcomed into some kind of club. It was a feeling about which I had mixed feelings.

But I thought no more of it until we were way out to sea, zooming along on this long slim rocket and I turned around from my spot at the sharp end and got a load of her. She had been below decks for a while, apparently changing, because she was now sitting in the middle of all the smiling studs way back there at the blunt end, in her new outfit, sipping a martini, laughing and chatting and completely, totally, stark frigging naked.

I was so surprised that I turned back around again to marshal my confusion, so to speak. I lay down again on my belly, chin on hands, watching flying-fish flying along in front of us. It was the first time I had seen flying-fish. It was also the first time I had seen any totally naked girl of mine shooting the shit with a bunch of drunken sailors. I didn't know what to think. Was this normal practice in these rarified circles, or was this a pre-arranged orgy? Was I about to be informed that I was in a porno movie, or was I on Candid Camera? After a while, I couldn't just lie there ignoring all this advanced sexuality without looking like the designated wanker at an orgy. So I strolled over, casual as you please, to join in whatever the fuck it was that was going on back there.

But they were all just as charming as before. Oh, hi! There you are! Having fun? Enjoying the boat? Want a drink? And is that an English accent are you just gay? I was greeted with smiles all around. They couldn't *stop* smiling. I was handed my drink, a rum and tonic as I recall, very yacht-club and not at all bad. So there we all were hoisting the old main-brace and splicing the old whatnot and all getting pleasantly shit-faced. But whatever it was we were all doing was just a strange, unspoken subtext to what was *really* going on, and what was really happening was that all eyes were crazy-glued to my baby's perfectly shaved little coochy.

I was in a crotchless romantic comedy. Every time she got up to walk around - and she not only walked around, she *sashayed* around, posing against the mast, lolling on ropes, practically frigging in the rigging - all eyes were on her. And she returned all the salivating stares with giggles and smiles. I was waiting for somebody to start throwing dollar bills at her.

We could have run aground. We could have hit a rare equatorial iceberg. Nobody would have noticed. They were all electrified. And I must say I was fascinated, too. Not just by this seagoing titty-bar vibe, but by the fact that nobody said anything about it. We just continued to make the most aimless of small talk. The weather. The wind. The stock market. Everything except my baby's winking slot. Nobody mentioned the fact that there was a nude sailorette sauntering among us with her pretty little labia fluttering in the trade winds. When would the bomb drop? When would these wealthy layabouts start howling like dogs and gang-shag her over the hand-rail? Were they waiting for a signal from me? Was this the kind of polite society where the groom has to go first, sort of thing? I was lost. I was at sea, so to speak. I *so* wanted to do the right thing and not look like the boorish landlubber, that I racked my brains but could find nothing in Edith Wharton to cover this particular eventuality. So I decided to beat a tactical retreat, flee the field and regroup. I excused myself and went below to take a long, unnecessary leak, thereby leaving them all to sort out their strange sexual semiotics.

And sure enough, while I was down there rolling a much-needed joint on the teak toilet seat, it all happened, just as I had predicted. Bedlam broke out on deck. There was a sudden stampede above my head like the thunder of goat hooves, just the sort of pounding sounds you would expect from a bunch of priapic yachtsmen dog-piling onto a sperm-lathered sex-goddess. And, strangely enough, I felt good about it. It was a relief, because at least this was behavior I could *understand*. I congratulated myself on having done the right thing in letting them all get on with it, instead of just standing around wondering which facial expression to adopt while my consort was being reamed by the fleet. I sat there for a long time, inhaling while sailing, and I spent every minute of it picturing all the scenarios that might confront me when I re-emerged, because I wanted to be prepared for absolutely anything so as to be able to carry it all off with the correct amount of *sang-froid,* or *savoir-faire* or whichever one of those French concepts might be called for. In fact, I decided that whatever was happening when I arrived back on deck, I would not only affect a slightly bored expression, I would join in. I would stroll up to the poop deck, take in the scene with a sardonic smirk and then utter the words that some of us have been waiting a lifetime to deliver, "Stand aside, lads. I'll be seventh. But I'm *damned* if I'll be last."

I finally poked my head above the hatch, fully expecting see her doing the breast-stroke in a lagoon of seamen's semen. But I was totally floored by what actually *was* going on.

Nothing was going on, nothing at all. All was just as before. There she still was, chatting and naked. There they all still were, chatting and drooling. The only change was that she was now sporting a lot more goose bumps and a pair of erect nipples you could hang your hat and coat on, but which were now pointing the way home instead of out to sea. All that banging and scrambling had simply been a burst of concerted action to turn the boat around, or to 'bring her about', as we say so suggestively out here on the heaving deep. We were headed back to Honolulu because the wind was turning nasty. In fact it was kicking up so fiercely now, we were practically surfing down the big waves and were docked and tied up before my imagination had time to calm down from its attack of unbridled filth.

In no time at all, she was happily singing along with the car radio as we sped along the Honolulu freeway and Smokey Robinson was having his usual calming effect on me, as was the joint we were passing back and forth, another one of those cerebral stool-softeners we chain-smoked up there on the Heights. But we weren't going back up there yet. No. We were on a mission.

Apparently, we were almost out of pot, a disaster of unimaginable scale. We still had a big bag of the evil shit up there on the hill, enough to fell a horse regiment, but you can never be too careful. God forbid we should be taken short and wind up accidentally straight for five minutes. After all, this was Hawaii, for the love of Krishna. This is why we were here in the first place, instead of that sweaty shit hole New Orleans. So my questions re the boys on the boat had to wait.

We swung off the freeway and were soon crawling through the cool and leafy boulevards of a very swank quarter indeed. If you were forced at gunpoint to live in a suburb, this might be the one. It was a slightly over-ripe version of Beverly Hills and way more exclusive. Insanely green lawns trimmed to within an inch of their lives nestled among palm-shaded flowerbeds of almost psychedelic color, in a paradise of humming-birds and hibiscus. It was as quiet, as safe, as tasteful and as subdued a display of insane wealth as you will find in these islands and as old as money gets around here. I had a feeling I was about to 'meet the folks'.

We cruised lazily along one lush avenue after another, until we came upon something so jarringly out of place that it seemed barely possible, considering the perfection all around us - not just the wealth, but the uniformity of tone, that aura of respectability that the very rich cultivate like a rare swamp orchid. Slap dab in the middle of this tropical fairy-land and ringed by a high chain-link fence, was what looked like a small private prison.

It was bizarre, a hideous eyesore that dominated the otherwise lordly avenue and took up an entire corner lot. The land alone must have been worth millions. What was it doing here? As we approached it, the most shocking detail was that chain-link fence. It was all the way out to the sidewalk and ran around the entire property six feet high and patrolled on the inside by a big, murderous mastiff. What the hell could this be? How could they have allowed such an outrage to exist in such a quilted, cream-puff neighborhood?

As we got closer I got a better look at the place. It was not a jail, it was just a very industrial-looking old bungalow, formerly the pride and joy of some rich family, but now stripped down and painted a drab battleship gray with all the windows blacked out and the shutters nailed shut. There were no flowers, no shrubs, no lawn, no songbirds, no butterflies, nothing but an expanse of bald dirt inside a heavily secured perimeter with a drooling hellhound loping around inside it. It was no longer a house. It was a compound. It hummed with criminal vibes. And it was right here in the middle of paradise, surrounded on all sides by lush, un-fenced gardens, curving, un-gated driveways, roses, bougainvilleas, miniature poodles and family values.

It was also a show of naked power. Somebody in there had some serious juice. Nobody could possibly want this sore thumb here in this manicured paradise. Everybody in the area must have tried to get rid of it, and these were not neighbors to be trifled with. These were some of the richest families in Hawaii. But clearly none of them had been able to do a damn thing about it. I asked my baby to slow down and stop alongside it so I could get a better look. It had a tall gate set into the fence, behind which the dog now started to growl at us in a scary baritone. 'Abandon hope all ye who enter here', I thought to myself. I turned around and said, "OK, I've seen it. Now let's get out of here." But she gave me a slightly pitying smile, and shook her head very slowly from side to side, causing her long hair to sway back and forth across those perfectly freckled breasts. "Don't be silly, Sweetie" she said. "We're here."

Here? I beg your pardon? You mean to say this was our actual *destination?* You mean we're going into that snake-pit? On *purpose?* Not at gunpoint? You mean you seriously intend to ask me to...

But she was already out of the car, skipping across the road, and the dog was already going ape-shit, sending great gobs of slobber flying off in all directions like coveys of flushed grouse. And now she was... oh, my God! She was *ringing the bell?* This was crazy. The dog was practically somersaulting with rage and literally throwing itself at the fence. She was going to get torn apart. Had she smoked one too many of those *pakalolo* spliffs and finally lost it? But she just turned around and smiled her sunniest, happiest smile, while about twelve inches behind her the man-eater kept roaring and hurling itself at the gate. *Smash! Smash!*

The gate could not hold that beast for long. I jumped out of the car, ran over to her and grabbed her hand to drag her away, but the creature suddenly stopped dead. Just like that. Silence and drool. Then I realized that somebody had signaled to it from the house and the dog had stopped mid-somersault. It turned and skulked over to the house, tail between legs, looking scared. The bungalow's front door was ajar and an extremely large man was standing in the doorway. He pushed it open a bit more to protrude further, and he filled it. He was enormous. He looked nastier than the dog. His legs were massive and tan below his surfer shorts, so were his arms, so was his tree-trunk neck. He was wearing a bandana on his head and an un-buttoned Hawaiian shirt over his huge chest. The dog went over to him and lay down at his feet, whimpering. The big guy put his hand on his hip and shifted his weight, and in doing so, pulled aside his shirt and exposed a big black object tucked into the waistband of his shorts. It was a handgun. A big one. Oh, sweet, bullet-riddled Jesus. My girl and I just stood there, holding hands and looking at him. One of us was trying very hard not to wet himself.

The big guy slowly cracked his stubbled face with a big evil grin, directed at us, reached back into the doorway with one huge hand and a loud *BUZZZZZ* went off right next to my ear. I nearly shat. The gate slowly swung open of its own weight. Oh, no. There was now *nothing between us and the dog.* Was he going to set it on us? It started rumbling from deep in its chest. It bared its fangs. It tensed all its muscles. It leaned forward on its hind legs, like a sprinter, waiting to fly at us, waiting for the signal to tear our throats out. I squeezed my sphincter even tighter to try and stop my imagination from running down my leg.

But the guy just kept smiling at us in that cold-blooded way. Next to me, I felt her tremble. I wanted to try to calm her but I was speechless and I was not about to take my eyes of that carnivore. Then she let go of my hand and I glanced sideways at her. She wasn't trembling at all. She was laughing. And then - Omigod - she was *running up the path,* straight at the guy. Whu? And the guy was standing there with his arms open wide and the dog was going bananas. She ran right up to him and jumped clear off the ground into his arms and he hugged her like a long-lost daughter and swung her around and around, and the dog suddenly lost interest in both of them and stared at me, only at me, growling louder and drooling more. Hey! Yo! *Helloooo!* Don't forget the dog! Excuse me? The dog? *Don't forget the fucking dog!*

Inside the house it was very dark. I was wedged into the corner of a fake leather sofa with the brute on the floor in front of me slobbering on my foot. It lay there and looked up at me with big brown eyes every bit as friendly as Sonny Liston's. I got the strong feeling that if I reached down to pat him, he would take my hand off at the wrist. The armed thug and my little pumpkin were horsing around together in the middle of the thick shag carpet. He was tickling her and making her giggle. She was punching his big belly and pinching his big hairy tits. She even grabbed his big gun with two hands and poked him in the gut with it. I shuddered and the dog growled. But he just laughed it off. "Aw, c'mon baby. Don't shoot. Hoo! Hoo! It ain't loaded, anyway. Haw haw!"

Suddenly, into this cuddly tableau tiptoed a tiny old Japanese lady. She was very prim, all smiles, dolled up in a fancy kimono-style house-coat and beaming with motherly pride at the joshing little TV episode in front of her. "Mama, Mama", shrieks my beautiful girl. "Well, lookee here!" smiles the little old lady from Okinawa. Even the dog gets up and ambles over to give everybody a lick and a crotch sniff, before coming back to his post in front of me with a fresh mouthful of drool. 'Mama' came and sat down next to me, all smiles. She put her tiny hand on my knee and asked me angelically if I was treating her favorite girl the way she deserved. Images of whips and handcuffs flew by as I assured her that yes, ma'am, I believed I was. The entire situation was becoming so warm and fuzzy I almost forgot that one of us was packing heat and the whole place had the feel of being targeted for an air-strike by the Feds. What the *McFuck* was going on here?

The big lug left the room with his gun in one hand and came right back with a large brick in the other. It was wrapped in aluminum foil. He tossed into my lap. It was heavy. Like a brick. Were we going to be asked to toss it through somebody's window? Was I now part of a gang? "What's this?" I asked him. "Maui Wowie," he said. Oh. Really? Marijuana? So this was just her *dealer?* Holy shit. See, when I go to score a little reefer, there's no artillery. Me and my local weed guy in New York have a nice glass of wine in his comfy little apartment that features a few primo custom guitars, and I stroll home with the merch in a cute little plastic baggie. This was different. This one-pound tinfoil brick felt like it had just been chain-sawed off a half-ton bale of export-grade hydroponic, prior to jungle airlift out.

As we drove away, the odd couple actually stood in the doorway and waved, all smiles, while the dog slobbered on the concrete and wagged its tail. I needed a drink. What the hell was my debutante mixed up in? In less than an hour we had gone from the family yacht to the Manson Family and she seemed to be equally at home in both. We turned back onto the freeway and headed home. She turned on Smokey Robinson and I turned it off again. "OK", I said, "Who are the Rotarians?"

She looked peeved and bored. She rolled those lovely eyes and shrugged those lovely shoulders and stared at the road. After a few minutes, she said,

- OK. I should have told you but I didn't know how you'd take it.
- Take what?
- My little secret.
- What little secret?
- I trick.
- You do what?
- I trick.
- OK. Show us a trick.
- No, dummy. I mean I *turn* tricks.
- You're a hooker?
- No I am *not* a hooker, for God's sake. That's *disgusting*.

She paused, looking offended.

- I'm a call-girl. You don't even know the difference, do you?
- Of course I do.

I paused, looking stupid.

- What's the difference?
- Well, a call-girl... Oh, for God's sake. It's like a sort of, you know,

like... an escort.

- Ah. So you *do* fuck guys for money.

- *No!* I do *not.*

- So what do you do, then?

- I fuck guys *for a whole lot* of money.

- Ah. That *is* different.

- Bingo, baby.

I followed her gaze down the road, trying to look like I was hip to such prostitutional nuance. We drove in silence for a few mystery miles.

- So who's the little old chick?

- The little old chick? (now she was really offended) That little old chick is a genius.

- Well, I'm sure she is, cupcake.

- *What?* Don't you patronize *me*, you... you *boy scout.*

I looked down at my lap.

- That little old chick is the biggest madam in Honolulu, possibly in the entire North Pacific region.

I now tried to look experienced in matters both pornographic *and* geographic.

- And the guy with the gun?

- Oh, for God's sake. The guy with the gun?

She said this in the patient tone one might use on a slow child.

- The guy with the gun is the guy with the gun. OK?

Well that did it. I may have been half in love with her already. But with that little Bogart gem tossed like a casual smoke ring, I was besotted. I tried very hard to control my desire to lean over and lick her like a puppy, but that would have definitely punctured the fabulous aura of *pulp noir* that suddenly hung around us like musk. Instead, I reached over and turned Smokey back on the radio. He was singing my favorite line from my favorite tune. *I love it when we're cruisin' together.* We cruised together into the sunset and back up onto the magic mountain.

Back at the ranch, back at the fabulous pad paid for not by her parents, but by her peerless pudenda, I was filled in on the details. Madam Mao, as I liked to think of her, owned several high floors in the fanciest high-rise on Waikiki Beach, which made her a real-estate mogul right there, even without the spectacular revenue stream that gushed from its wildcat drillings day and night, especially night. Little by little, my baby fed me details of the larger velvet painting, little glimpses of that fabulous floating world that is always among us, lodged between the laminates of what we rubes think is the real one, curling around our grasp of reality like cigar smoke. At the end of a long night of personal illumination and as the dawn was warming our heavy eyelids, I asked her one last question and hated myself for it, the moment it left my lips.

 - And... the boys on the boat?
She frowned slightly and let slip a sigh not so much of vexation as of disappointment. She was about to tell me, when I came to my senses and touched my fingers to her lips.

 - The boys on the boat... are the boys on the boat?
She turned towards me on the pillow and gave me one of those crooked smiles you dream about, and whispered,

 - Bingo, Baby.
Then she rolled over and fell asleep.

Well, well. I'll be dipped in shit. Living off immoral earnings? Great. Doing so unbeknownst? Embarrassing. But all I could think about as I mulled it over was 'How?' How could we possibly live so intimately and I not know? Oh, don't get me wrong, I'm all for prostitution, if only on the principle that *anything* is better than actual work. But how was her fee-based fornication physically possible, time-wise? She was never gone for more than an hour and it was a fifteen-minute drive each way. How could she trick her way to the bank in thirty minutes, tops? The answer, it turned out, was the Japanese Business Fuck.

With very little prodding she did her impersonation of the JBF. It was all business. The bow. The mount. The quick bang bang. The grunt. The dismount. The bow. The exit. Just like that. In and out, so to speak. But to give the bonsai boys their due, they did come here by the jumbo-jet-load primarily to play *golf,* damn it. So they simply played her the way they played the *other* eighteen holes, with the fewest strokes possible.

So for the next few weeks, in the warm twilight, we would raise our glasses to Mitsubishi and Matsushita and Mantovani and all the other members of the economic miracle that had made our lives so miraculous. Then one day, with my unerring talent for the wrong move, it occurred to me that I should get up off my pampered ass and visit the rest of Hawaii. Why? I have no idea. Why do we do these things? Why is it that anything, absolutely anything, can start to feel a wee bit tired after a while, even a daily tongue-bath from a highly trained professional? I have come to the conclusion that the answer lies in the general direction of *Satan.*

She pouted a bit, but I went my idiot way on the understanding that I would be back soon. Oh, I had all manner of nifty adventure, most of it behind the best psilocybin mushrooms that ever grew out of cow shit, so most of it is a blur, but I do remember walking on sugar-white sands, catching sight of myself in rock pools and realizing that I was at some peak of gilded youth, brown as a coconut, healthy as a horse, hair to my shoulders, with an angel waiting for me over the rainbow on her enchanted isle. What a feeling. But then one night while I was asleep under the stars on a Maui beach, the old '59 Volvo apparently decided that enough was enough and it was payoff time for the ingrate. My string of dumb luck had run its course, in fact the whole ball of string was about to unravel and I was now to be on my own, cut loose from the warp and weft of outrageous good fortune. It had all begun to unspool the day I handed over the *Vulva's* key to that last pretty woman and lost the key to an entire *world* of pretty women. The good time I'd been having was just borrowed time, and now the final strand suddenly came loose.

In my sleep, I rolled over onto a virus-riddled scorpion and the bastard stung me. And that was that. My idyll was like, er, *over,* dude.

I flew back to Honolulu in the local hospital plane, so ill that the cab driver had to carry me to bed, literally. My angel was sweet to me at first. We both thought I would recover at any minute and resume the old gavotte, but I didn't. I got sicker and sicker and she got sourer. After a week or so of not getting either shagged or shellacked, she explained to me that she wasn't really cut from the Florence Nightingale cloth and since she had never signed up for the old sickbed scenario, I should leave. Just like that. The angel threw me out. I was too weak even to protest. The next day, the very same cabbie who had carried me back to her scented bed carried me in his arms into the Honolulu YMCA.

The revenge of the car. That's what it was, pure and simple. They will *do* that, you know. You do *not* fuck with your bitch magnet. The Ford giveth. The Ford taketh away. But I was so horribly ill that I was actually relieved to be left to rot in peace. And boy, did I rot. After a few weeks of drifting in and out of fever and hallucination, crawling to my toilet and back, I woke up one day and felt better. I knew I was better because I wanted ice cream. I shuffled over to the mirror and was shocked by my reflection. In the intervening month or so I had grown a full beard. My lips were deeply fissured and black. My teeth were almost lost behind a wall of lumpy crud. I tested it with my long, filthy fingernails and it felt a quarter of an inch thick. I shuddered to think what my breath smelled like. My shoulder-length hair was matted and shining with grease and hung over my face in thick rasta ropes. I tried to brush it aside, but it was cemented in place and kept falling back like prison bars across my hollow cheeks. The general effect, the overall look, was that of a recently exhumed corpse.

I knew I should do something about my appearance before going out in public, but where would I start? And anyway, I didn't have the strength for that kind of frivolity. I needed ice cream. I simply had to take my living-dead act on the road and hope I didn't bump into any old gent with a nervous condition or an implanted fibrilator. I also decided to take a wide berth around children and horses.

I managed to put on my clothes and sunglasses, swayed down the hallway on my flip-flops, out into the blistering heat and along the glaring sidewalk. The noon furnace nearly knocked me over but I managed, by holding onto walls, to make it, swaying, to the end of the block and into a supermarket. It was freezing in there and it felt good. I lifted my head up to look around for the ice cream section and noticed that there were long strands of colored paper looped around everything and I started to hallucinate Christmas carols. Then it hit me. It really *was* Christmas. Holy tropical Jesus. I had totally forgotten. It's fucking *Christmas,* man. Oh joy. O little fucking town of Bethlehem.

I lurched the several intervening miles to the ice cream display, way over there in the cold section, near Vladivostok. To add to my terrifying general appearance, I noticed that I was now visibly shivering. I leaned into the yawning ice cave to make my Christmas selection. Pistachio Mint? Caramel Ripple? Vanilla Fudge? My mind was struggling with these poetic non-sequiturs, when my ruminations were rudely interrupted by a loud "Hey! Buddy!"

I reconvened my scattered wits sufficiently to realize that somebody was addressing me. I was helped in my deductive reasoning by the hand on my shoulder. "Hey, Buddy!" There it was again. I pictured a security guard wanting to know if this *actual zombie* could actually pay for his purchase or just wanted to lie down and chill out in this indoor snow bank. But as I turned around, I was greeted by a fat man's beaming face. Not a guard at all. A civilian. A civilian with a smile. It was a smile tinged with concern and flecked with sprinkles of doubt.

- Son, are you a...a Christian?

I tried very hard to tussle with this question, if only for my own edification. I reached deep into my storehouse of personal knowledge, but could come up with only one image - Santa Claus, nailed to a cross, encircled by a dozen Jewish-looking elves on their knees looking up at him, palms pressed together singing, 'Have Yourself A Merry Little Christmas'. But then I realized that it was just the supermarket soundtrack, and Dean Martin, dear old Dino, was just wishing all us hipsters a cool yule.

- Son? Are you with me? Can you understand what I'm saying?
I stood up a bit straighter and stared at him through my curtain of crud.
- Er....
- Oh, of course he can, honey. Here, let *me* talk to him.
The fat man's face was replaced by a fat woman's face.

- Young man, can I ask you a question?
- Er....
- Do you... do you have a place to stay?

Wait a minute. Whoah, Nelly. Ah ha! So! So *that* was it! I knew it! Even in my stupor, I could intuit the scenario. So! I had not entirely lost my studly appeal, eh? Oh, sure, I was a little grubby and not quite as vivacious as I might wish, but I still clearly had what it took to spark the interest of a red-blooded American woman, even one in her sixties, God bless her, the sporty old porker. Ah, yes, I could picture it now, riding off to their home among the palm trees to get bathed and shaved and to re-emerge as the bronzed young god that I really was beneath this coating of tooth crud and shit-encrusted ass-hair. Your instincts are *correct*, ma'am. You can spot talent. I'll have you know that I was recently a pampered boy toy, servicing a real *corker* of girl, let me tell you. Don't worry, Sir. I'll have that old babe walking like John Wayne in two shakes! I'm your man. Ready when you are. Saddle her up, James. Just let me dust off my rusty scrotum and we'll pole-vault together into the sunset.

- Son?
- Er...?
- Son, as you may know, it's Christmas. And around this time of year, we usually like to go out, my husband and I do, and find someone like yourself. What we are looking for is a truly needy case, someone who is *really* hopeless. And this year, well... we've chosen you.
- You... You whu...?

I tried to get a word out, but she hushed me with a white-gloved hand and, with a smile full of love for all creatures great, small and shit-encrusted, she thrust a few neatly folded bills into my hand. Her husband beamed on, over her perfumed shoulder.

- Whu...? You mean...?
- That's alright, son. No need to thank us. We know how grateful you must feel, *you poor thing*.

They turned away and I stared after them as they waddled off together, holding hands and turning the corner from Dairy Products into Sliced

Meats. I sat down on the edge of the freezer as if pushed down by force, and looked at my shaking hands through my vile stalactites of greasy filth. In my left hand there were about thirty or forty dollars folded neatly and smelling of soap. In my right there was a pint of ice cream. Rocky Road, as I recall. Very apt. On the lid there was a sticker with bright words dancing around in red and green, surrounded by a festive pattern of holly. I raised it up to my stupefied face and read it.

It said, 'Hey there! Feeling Lucky? Well guess what! You may already be... *A WINNER!!!*'

FANCY A SNACK?

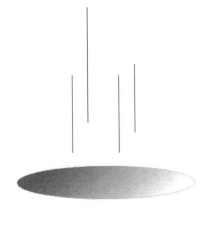

CAMBODIA

I was living in Phnom Penh, on the riverfront, in a roof apartment with a great view of the two great rivers coming together, the mighty Mekong merging with the Tonlé Sap, two different shades of brown, two different flavors of monsoon mud bleeding together like shot silk and rolling slowly away downhill together like Jack and Jill, interlaced and glinting and half a mile wide, down to Vietnam and to the vast unknowable Mekong Delta and the piratical South China Sea.

The rains were over, the sky was blue and the promenade of outdoor cafes were awash in sidewalk tables packed with people glad to see the sun again and getting nicely tweaked on Cambodia's hilariously named Happy Pizza. 'Happy' means 'with marijuana.' Extremely strong marijuana. Strong enough to make a simple visit to the toilet feel like you're bringing a 747 in to land.

I sat down at an outside table on my first day there, watching the third river, the one of bicycles and tricycles and motor scooters and very pretty girls who smile at you so frankly that it makes you wonder, until you've been there a few more days and you stop wondering, because it's, you know, all *perfectly clear.*

- Excuse me?
- Yes sir.
- This happy pizza…
- Yes sir.
- Well I love the 'happy' part, but I don't really feel like a pizza.
- Oh, no problem sir. We can make *anything* happy here.
- You can?
- Oh, yes, sir.
- Anything?
- Oh yes.
- How about the fish?
- Oh. We can make your fish happy, sir. No problem.
- Amazing.
- Oh, yes. How happy would you like your fish?
- I don't really know.
- Little bit happy? Medium happy? *Very happy* fish?
- I think I would like a medium happy fish.
- OK, sir.
- Not too happy, you understand.
- No sir.
- Just… *cheerful,* know what I mean?
- Whatever you say, sir. One medium happy fish, coming right up.
- Fantastic.
- Oh yes, sir. *Very* fantastic.

The café was next door to my building. On a lower floor, there was a young guy named Davit, a good-looking Khmer I used to hang out with. Davit was immodestly proud of his English, specifically of his fine stash of off-hand phrases, casually delivered.

There were not so many and he used them all so often that I think I've remembered all of them. They were, as I recall, in no particular order;

Fancy a snack?

What's up, Doc?

No way, Jose!

Cool your jets!

Go figure

I kid you not.

Kiss my ass.

Whatever, man.

Eat shit.

She fucks like a rabbit.

Check, please!

Yes, that was about it, the entire list as I remember it. Not many. But it was absolutely *astonishing* how many he could worm into any conversation. Here's a conversation I remember vividly, because I've been over it in my head so often. Classic Davit, in every way. One night I had loaned him five dollars for an hour or two with his favorite rent-girl and I bumped into him later in a bar.

- What's up, Doc?
- So! How was it, Davit?
- She fucks like a rabbit. She's crazy about me, man. Tonight I made her come so many times she gave me my money back. *I kid you not.*
- Wow. Nice going. So. Hand it over.
- No way, Jose.
- What do you mean?
- I *earned* that five dollars.
- No, you didn't. *She* earned it. Then she gave it back to you.
- Go figure.
- But I gave you the five dollars that she gave back to you.
- Cool your jets. The five you gave me and the five she gave me?
- Yeah? What?
- Not the same five dollars.

- Well, I'll be dipped in shit!

- Whatever, man. Check please!

One sunny afternoon, he asked me, casual as you please, if I'd 'fancy a snack'. Now, on most occasions this would have been an innocent enough question and just another chance to show off his idiomatic snazz. But this time it was delivered a wee bit too casually for the trained eye. It was the imperceptibly raised eyebrow that gave the bastard away. That arched brow was something I was always on the lookout for with Davit, because the one *other* thing he took immodest pride in was watching my face when I was presented with the vilest shit ever seriously offered as food. Slug. Sparrow. Bowel. Eye.

I kid you not. The last time he'd asked me if I fancied a snack, the 'snack' had jumped off my fork into my shirt pocket. It was a live shrimp. But I ate the fucker anyway. He knew I would. He knew that I would always eat it whatever it was, whatever it *looked* like or *stank* like or - God help us - *twitched* like. He knew that whatever face I might pull as I steered the latest outrage down my incredulous pie-hole, it *would* go down. Eventually. I wouldn't give him the satisfaction of an actual balk. And, thus far, my batting average had been perfect. I had eaten everything. And it tickled him no end, the sense of honor with which I stuck to my gustatory guns. My position, basically, was that I would eat anything that would not eat me first. Period. And he was proud of me in the same way one might be of a pet ferret that would go down *any* rabbit hole.

And yet. And yet. Oh, I don't know. There was something in that fiendish cocktail of the innocent question and the diabolically raised eyebrow that told me that *this* time, maybe *this* time, whatever hellish organism he was going to set in front of me, this time it just might not, you know, *stay* down.

Oh, what the hell. We set off on our funky old motorbikes. We were headed for an obscure spot upstream, on the banks of the Mekong, in the woods, a strictly Khmer-only sort of place. I was supposed to feel honored. I felt queasy.

A narrow red-dirt road followed the wide river, with occasional houses on its banks, then shacks, then just woods. We wheeled off onto a little track that ended right at the river's edge in a clearing full of sun. The restaurant was true Khmer style. In other words, there was *nothing there.* No tables, no chairs, no cushions, no plates, no cutlery, no walls. Just an empty platform with reed mats on it, a roof overhead made of palm leaves, and a few low-slung hammocks, inches off the ground. The food was served on banana leaves, and you lolled in your hammock and scooped it up languorously with your fingers like an orangutan. Doing it felt somehow unutterably luxurious.

The sun came down through the trees in shafts that moved slowly over the slow muddy water, water the color of a chestnut racehorse that has just run all the way from China. It was one of those spots where you suddenly feel an ineffable rush of being very *very* far away.

Downriver a little, beached on the mud of the riverbank, was the rotting hulk of a big old riverboat, solid teak, pale grey with age, falling apart slowly and gracefully, showing its elegant ribs like a dead beast in the desert, at rest among the bright green reeds and framed by the big brown river. As we drank our beers and said nothing, swinging in our hammocks, the old riverboat shape-shifted into my own recurring-dream-boat, with shiny teak floors, bamboo shades, paper lanterns, ceiling fans going slowly around and maybe a nice skinny brown bride inside there somewhere with shiny black hair, lolling across a silk divan under a mosquito net draped like the eaves of a Siamese palace, a modest little floating Xanadu. But it was suddenly sunk by a *real* girl with shiny black hair, our waitress, a pretty little thing with a huge basket on her head, so big that we had to help her down with it. Uh oh. So here it came. This was it. Lunch, God help me. My sphincter clenched. Maybe audibly.

Inside the big basket there were two large mounds covered with different colored cloths. She threw back the first one with a flourish. I gasped. Or I yelped. I can't remember the exact noise. It was possibly closer to a whimper. There in front of me was my own personal culinary Armageddon - the one thing I had prayed I would never have to place on my tongue. Spiders. Not itsy bitsy ones, either. Big fat Tarantulas, four or five inches around and thick as hockey pucks, big juicy creepy crawlies covered in matted black fur and with their long, hairy legs gathered around them like some nightmarish garnish. They might be considered beautiful on the Discovery Channel, but cooked and for lunch? Sweet barfing Jesus, do I *have* to do this? If ever anything did not want to be food, this was it.

I could feel the Davit eyebrow being raised beside me, accompanied by a barely suppressed titter. You bastard. Fancy a snack? Yeah, I fancy a snack. How about *your liver?* But the thing is that, horrible as they were, I would have had a crack at these big black gag bombs, just to wipe that smirk of his face. Unfortunately, I had met a guy named Dude.

Dude, or Dudley in the long version, was a wandering American and a master of the non sequitur. Like...

- Dude, what did you do back in the States?
- What did I *do?* My dad owns an engineering company.

We had met a few weeks earlier in Battambang, a town notorious for being the last holdout of the Khmer Rouge. Battambang is nothing much, but it sits on a beautiful bend in the river in a vast plain of rice paddies which when I arrived were so psychedelically green I thought I might have a brain tumor. They were so bionically green they actually glowed in the night, an emerald sea, visible from space, endless green fields, the killing fields. Yes, *those* killing fields.

Just a few years earlier, thousands of people had been bludgeoned to death in these fields for working not quite hard enough, because they were inconveniently dying of starvation. This was Pol Pot's ocean of green gold, upon which he sought to float his fanciful, lunatic experiment to wipe out all history and start over at Year Zero. Right here. And despite the exquisite erasure of this annual carpet quivering prettily all the way to the edge of the world, you would always wonder, with every old guy you met here, over a glass of green tea or a green cheroot, 'were *you* the guy who stove their heads in with a rock, or were you just the one who pushed them into the mass grave? Just wondering.

No big deal. *Whatever,* man.

Anyway, young Dude truly had eaten everything you can eat in Cambodia, living or dead or rented by the hour. And his judgment on everything was always the same. Everything was 'Pretty nice, pretty nice.' I asked him specifically about the spiders and he said they were 'Pretty nice, pretty nice.' But then after a pause he added, 'Pretty nice, but... see, you gotta understand, that when you bite into that big fat body, its kinda like biting into *a big sac of pus.'*

Oh. Yes. Well. See, now *right there* would be a problem, right there with the old sac o' pus business. Now, I'm not finicky. I will chew the head off that sauteed sparrow quick as the next guy. And I would have had a go at a spider, too, just to say that I *had*. I would have, until Dude unburdened himself of that one colorful phrase. The icky look of the things? Fine. The little hairy legs tickling your chin as you ate them? No problem. The big sac of pus? *Check, please!*

This vivid piece of oral cinema was presented for my consideration by Dude over a light dinner of bat, as in belfry. It was 'pretty nice', as I recall, washed down with big tin bowls of rice wine. Bat was a delicacy peculiar to one very peculiar establishment - a gambling den full of loudly yelling drunks playing a game that seemed to depend on one's ability to drink more, scream more and bang on the table more than one's opponent. As a result, the whole rickety joint was waving drunkenly on its bamboo stilts at the edge of this green sea of waving grain, this obscenely beautiful palimpsest of unnatural history.

And now here I was on the Mekong, in another little unnatural eatery: Chock Full O' Bugs. I pulled myself together as much as I could and looked over towards Davit, the sniggering bastard, swinging in his hammock a few feet from me in the restaurant's 'smirking section'. I tried to give him a look not of horror, but one of profound disappointment. *'Spiders,* Davit?' I said, as one might say, looking down one's nose, Beaujolais *Nouveau?*

It was a desperate move, but it worked. He pulled a face and shrugged. - You're right. Spiders suck. I kid you not. Cool your jets. We'll eat the grasshoppers instead.

And on that signal, the girl threw back the *other* cloth and I nearly fell out of my frigging hammock. Under the other cloth was a mound of giant, glistening grasshoppers, even bigger than the spiders, four inches long, easy, and deep fried but with all their tiniest features intact. So they were all bug-eyed and *staring at you,* with long feelers and with big hind legs that had hairs on them and massive heads that had - god help us - *teeth.* They actually looked *worse than the spiders.* They were not of this planet. The escape from fat tarantula to giant grasshopper was about as comforting as climbing out of a cesspool only to be pelted with shit. Hey, don't eat *that* shit! Eat *this* shit!

The girl shoveled a hillock of these shiny extraterrestrials onto the floor between our two hammocks. Oh, my God. That glinting armor. Those *teeth.* Those ghoulish grins on their big bald heads. They were like grinning little stormtroopers out of *Alien.* I've eaten crickets in Bangkok, crispy little things, deep fried in sesame oil and, if you're drunk enough, they taste just like rice crackers. but these? There were big enough to have *opinions,* and vicious-looking enough to *bite you back.*

Davit, clearly unaware of the titanic war of the worlds going on between me and these horrifying beasts, nonchalantly picked one of them off the top of the heap, held it by its huge back legs and with a certain lazy grace, cavalierly bit its head off and chewed it. It made a crackling noise, the kind of noise one spends a lifetime *trying to forget.* The second bite ended in the middle of its armor-plated belly and the third left him holding just the two hairy hind legs, which he then tossed over his shoulder with great panache into the dappled waters of the mighty Mekong, which apparently had rolled all the way from China just to receive them. Then he inclined his head towards the heap of beady-eyed upchuck with all the delicacy of a Versailles courtier, as if to say 'Go ahead. Help yourself. Tuck in. *Indulge.'* I looked at him and said, - Davit, baby? Cool your jets. Fancy a snack? *No way, Jose!* Eat shit? *Kiss my ass.* I kid you not. *Check please!'*

SUPERHEROES
OF MASTURBATION

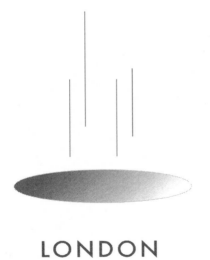

LONDON

I can write about this now because it happened so long ago that the embarrassment is no longer so excruciating.

I had moved in with a girl who was about to graduate from London University, as I had the previous year. We were both still just kids. It was a grandiose Victorian flat in a genuinely aristocratic enclave of the Royal Borough of Kensington, on a high floor overlooking the royal park and the huge round wedding cake of the Royal Albert Hall. All unutterably posh and expensive.

And there I was, overlooking all this gaudy regality, enthroned and enthralled. These were digs beyond my wildest dreams, beyond anybody's unless you were royalty, and her mother was, sort of, or near enough. I was so out of place there that I always felt like the young burglar who has been caught, but due to his youth and charm, has been let off, then taken in by the parents on a whim, given the run of the place and, amazingly, allowed to fuck the beautiful daughter. I'm sure there's a movie like this out there somewhere. Possibly French.

It was all implausibly majestic, built at a time of real imperial grandeur. The huge flat had corridors and arches. A thing you pulled in the parlor rang a bell in the faraway kitchen to alert the servants, although there were no actual servants any more, just an Irish maid who came in a few days a week and called everybody Sir and Madam. Everybody but me.

You could swing a panther in the pantry. You took an elaborate wrought iron lift down to a vast marble foyer that was actually designed for horses and carriages to drive through with enough room to pass each other. You were accompanied in this Jules Verne contraption by a slightly muted version of Sergeant Pepper. The Mother seldom showed up, which was a Good Thing because she was Rather Frightening. She herself had moved into even more baronial digs, thanks to a new husband of obscene wealth.

It was Saturday, the day the Mother always spent with the Beautiful Daughter, shopping, tea-drinking, and assassinating my character. My girlfriend would report Mama's latest opinion of me, imitating her theatrical style and waving an imaginary cigarette holder as a prop. " Yes, he has a certain charm, I suppose, but little or no job. Or perceptible future. And shagging my daughter is *not* a career, darling."

On this particular Saturday afternoon I watched my sweetheart take the usual long walk with her lovely rueful smile down the long hallway as she left to meet her maker. At the distant door she gave me the usual blown kiss and a wink followed by the usual hike of the very short skirt over the usual no panties. As usual, I could hear her still tittering as she was lowered grandly to the street, a lovely bird in a gilded cage.

I walked back to our enormous bedroom, formerly her mother's, pulled off all my clothes and arranged the camera and the tripod, and then onto the enormous bed I emptied the brown paper bag full of little bendable toy action-figures. They were little plastic superheroes - Silver Surfer, Spiderman, Batman, a whole bunch of them - purchased that very morning. I was ablaze with creativity on a new art project that would shut her mother up for good, an absolute *corker* of an idea that could not fail to make me a star in the art world.

I intended to shoot a series of photographs of these famous little characters, one at a time, from my own POV, each one facing away from me, sitting with their little bendy legs bent around my stiff cock, as if riding it into battle. It seemed like a terrific idea. *At the time.*

I intended it as a sardonic comment on that whole comic-book, heavy-metal cock-rock crap that everyone was into. Ever since I first thought of it, I had been tickled pink and cackling to myself, openly. It was a winner for sure. I even had a title. Superheroes of Masturbation. I couldn't wait to get started, without the girlfriend sitting around pissing herself with laughter at the sight of my stiff dick with a small plastic Superman perched on it. This was no time for distraction. This was serious stuff. This was Art. This was My Future.

I started in on the project, first arranging the pillows into a great stack so that I could gaze downwards to judge the exact angle of dangle, thereby calculating the anticipated inclination of inflation once I had emptied the *other* brown paper bag, the one full of porno magazines. Well, I thought I might need a little help.

I scattered them across the bed. Hmmm. Let me see now. *Barely Legal, Teen Titty, Teeny Cheeks, Young Snatch.* Hard to choose, really. I flipped through the glossy pages, browsing the blandished beaver and clocking the semiotics of teen filth; the school uniforms, the thumb-sucking, the coy smiles, the pigtails, the tooth-braces, the ankle socks, the cotton panties, the toes pointed inwards, the entire visual vocabulary of the knowing nubile, always looking upwards at the camera from beneath lowered lids as if to say, "Oh, sir, oh sexy sir, we are all so very naughty. Do with us what you will." Embarrassing, really. Exploitative, definitely. But it worked like a charm. In no time at all I was stiffer than a statutory rape sentence and starting to position the first of the little action figures athwart the resultant chubby.

I envisioned a very limited edition of very large photographs. Tiny plastic heroic figurines astride the old stiffy, straddling it bareback into galactic combat – Captain America, Green Lantern, Batman, the whole nutty crowd, one at a time, all spurring on my droll wood into art legend.

There would be a storm-cloud background, of course, of a heroic, Wagnerian / Marvel Comics ilk that I could add in at some point, details to be worked out later. I was too busy at this juncture mentally fast-forwarding to the unveiling on opening night. The gasps, the applause, the laughter, the scandal, the fame, the teenage groupies, the white cotton panties, the coy smiles, the toes pointed inwards.

My scandalous new *oeuvre,* which would already have been whispered of in concentric circles, would be mounted high around a vast room - one of those agoraphobic art hangars humming with the obscenity of wasted space. The huge first-night crowd would be craning to get a load of this serio-comico-porno piece of public art starring my private part and a bagful of plastic toys. The whole thing was such a fabulous idea that my art fame was not only assured, it was imminent.

So there I was setting up the first shot on my trajectory into the pantheon: Wonder Woman straddling the, ahem, *vehicle,* her little bendy legs bent around it and one tiny arm thrust upwards in a pose of warlike spleen. The effect was staggering in its crypto-femino-farcico smut. Oddly poignant. Comically filthy.

I shot a few snaps that I was delighted with and was in the process of reaching for The Incredible Hulk, to give him his fifteen in the spotlight - I pictured him standing foursquare among the vine-like pubery, arms raised in awe at the hilarious obelisk - when my eyes strayed over the pile of splayed teen loin glinting winsomely on the bed beside me. Hmmm. That one particular little shaved coochy, poking over the rim of those pulled-down panties. Poking? Winking, more like. Oh, you naughty child. Why, Daddy just might have to wipe that vertical smile off those naughty little lips and give baby a petite little spanky... wanky...

*   *   *   *   *

I was aware of a muffled shriek. I felt a kick in the ribs. I yelped. I opened my eyes. Standing over me, was the Rather Frightening Mother, like an eagle fallen on a mouse. She was fairly *sputtering* with rage.

- What the... bloody hell is... *going on* back here?

- Whu? *Agnes?* What are *you* doing here?

She was standing glowering over me, arms akimbo I believe is the correct term.

- What am *I* doing here? What the hell are *you*...doing...here?

I woke up in a split sec. and surveyed the scene. Oh, sweet self-abusing Jesus. Hairless teen slot all over the show. Barely legal labiae and ani just pouting pitilessly all around. Even worse, Wonder Woman was suspended from my now-limp dicklet, hanging on for dear life, one little painted plastic leg stuck into a puddle of suspiciously viscous opalescence that had pooled among the pubes, my one hand still sleepily holding the glossy representation of a plump young twat, the other guiltily a-glint with pearly ejaculate.

- Oh, God, Agnes. This must look like...

- Look *like?* It doesn't look *like* anything. Obviously I've just walked in
    on a... a... .a highly elaborate... *wank!*

I slid slowly off the big stack of pillows and hit the bed, *her* bed, with a long groan, pulling on my jeans and surreptitiously wiping my hand underneath a pillow, *her* pillow. I mumbled into it.

- When did you get back?

- Just now. We bought you a cake for a treat, you... you dirty little twerp.

- Oh, God. Where is she?

- She's in the kitchen, making tea, poor thing.

- She didn't see this, did she?

- No, thank God, poor lamb. She sent me back here to get you. She
    thinks you're actually *busy* with some *art* thingy.

- I *am* busy with it, Agnes. I am. This is it. This is the *thingy.* This is...this
    is... goddamn it, Agnes, this is *art.*

- Oh, *excuuuuse* me. I'm terribly sorry. I mistakenly thought that what
    with the bed being covered in photographs of shaved...you know what,
    and with your hand on your willy, and a small puddle of spermatozoa
    slathered all over your little toy rubber dolly...

- It is *not a dolly!*

- Oh, I'm sorry. Have I insulted... *her?*

- Agnes, this is a well-known character from the comic book culture of which you know nothing at all, of course, but which is itself a sort of ontological index of disaffected mainstream art, or symbol thereof. Sort of thing.

- Of course it is, dear. And the masturbation? Is a symbol of what, exactly? Unbridled filth?

- Oh, god.

- My poor daughter. If I were she I wouldn't touch you with a...a... disinfected *stick,* you furtive little perv.

- Agnes. I'm begging you to give me the benefit of the doubt here.

- Oh I do, dear. Why, that must be aloe vera you've squirted on her, to bring out the *shine.*

- Agnes. Pleeeease.. I'm begging you.

- Begging for what? Kleenex?

- Agnes, I know you're having fun torturing me like this. But this is an actual *project,* damn it. Look. See? The camera.

- Aaarrrgghh!!! *Cameras?* Oh, dear God. Is there no *end* to your pervy ways? Must we now all confront your genitalia in our living rooms *on the telly?*

- It's just set up to make art photos, Agnes. This is *art,* damn it. I'm doing a series of comic-erotic works. I have a gallery that's expressed interest and I was just in the middle of it and I got a little...OK... well... distracted, I'll admit, and then I must have dozed off. It's all very embarrassing, OK? But it's art, Agnes. It's *actual art.* Don't you see? Look, I've got the original proposal right here somewhere underneath these magazines...

- Aaargghh! - Don't *touch* those disgusting things! Good God. What sort of girls *show* that, anyway? Not exactly shy, are they? Are their parents still with us, do you suppose? Good lord, I haven't even seen *my own* that clearly. And what is it with all this shaving business down there? Look at it. It looks like chemotherapy. Oh, put them away. All those bald vaginas are putting me off my *cake.*

- Agnes. Please hear me out...

- My poor daughter. You should be ashamed of yourself. There she is, studying for her degree *like a fiend,* and here *you* are lying around all day just...*playing with yourself?*

- Damn it, Agnes, I was not playing with myself. Well, briefly, maybe. But this is work. It's art.

- I *beg* your smutty little pardon? What did you say? *Work?!*

- Yes. I did say that. Agnes, this is work. It's actual work!

- Work? Did you dare to say *work?*

She arched one perfectly penciled eyebrow, as only she could, took an audible intake of breath and let fly with her zinger.

- If this is work, young man, then all I can say is that you've got a *fucking good union!*

And with that, she turned on her tastefully midsized heel and swanned out of the room grandly, followed by her own personalized cloud of perfumed umbrage. She went to re-join her poor, misguided daughter in the kitchen and to leave me to stew in my own - you'll excuse the word - juice.

I LIKE YOUR THIGHS

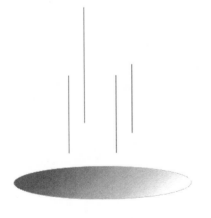

HONG KONG

Traveling alone is a singular experience in more ways than one. Aloneness attracts the weird. It is also a magnet for the dim, the unhinged and the recently escaped. By simply *booking* a ticket for one, you already bear a scarlet letter invisible to all but the certifiable. Strangeness that will avoid you like the plague if you are part of a couple or group will, the moment you go solo, stick to you like shit to a blanket. When you travel in a party, strangers talk to you. When you go it alone, strange *people* talk to you.

For instance, in the 80s I was on a bus that was ferrying passengers from the old Hong Kong Airport into Kowloon, which in those days was Hong Kong's most criminally overcrowded quarter, a place that could make Dante flinch. I had just flown in from Bangkok. I mention that it was the *old* airport I had just touched down in so that those familiar with it might have some idea of the nervous state I was already in when the fruitcake I was about to meet barged into the itinerary.

If you are familiar only with the *new* Hong Kong Airport, the one that rejoices in the highly suggestive name Chek Lap Koc, I should point out the difference between this spiffy new hub and the old one. A landing at the new Hong Kong airport is like arriving at the Pearly Gates on a fluffy white cloud while angels blow in your ear. Chek Lap Koc, naughty name notwithstanding, is spotless, stainless and peerless, a tongue-bath for the traveler, thoughtfully placed on an island far away from the shiny shit-heap of the metropolis. From the new airport, one is effortlessly beamed into downtown, cushioned within a noiseless sky-train via a series of elegant bridges and tunnels. It is an ethereal experience, almost a destination in itself.

The old place was very far, in every way, from that. Those unfortunate enough to remember the *old* airport, may already be experiencing an involuntary constriction of the rectal muscles at its very mention. Put simply, a landing at the *old* airport, especially in a jumbo jet, was an exercise in anal continence in the face of overwhelming odds *against*.

For a start, the old airport was practically *in* Kowloon, where there was reportedly one person per square foot and they all had very small feet. Picture Kennedy Airport crammed into Central Park and you'll get the picture. No, Wait. Move that over into East Harlem and you'll get the picture *and* the cast. Crumbling old apartment buildings, seething with humanity and festooned with wet washing, butted right up against the old runway, damn near scraping the wingtips off the 747s. They were laid out in row upon row, like a suicide regiment of urban squalor alongside the *actual runway*. And this was the busiest airport in Asia. So there was always a long line of jumbos waiting for take-off, taxiing slowly past all this, every plane packed with passengers staring out from the window-seats, appalled, getting a load of these ant-heaps and all experiencing a phobia that none of them knew existed before this moment; the fear of *not flying*.

And that was just the backdrop. Then there was the runway itself. Over the years, as planes got bigger, the runway had been made progressively longer to give them enough room to take off and land.

But the airport was on the water's edge *to begin with.* So they had no choice but to keep building it further out into the sea. The bigger the planes got, the further out went the runway. By the time the era of the jumbo arrived, the end of the runway was so far out it was among the shipping lanes. Pilots of 747s would practically have to *stand* on the brakes to stop their big fuel-bombs from crashing into the sides of container ships as big as small cities. And on either side of this airstrip, sloshing up against the whole length of it, was the septic tank known as Hong Kong Harbor, full of shit and sharks. So there was no margin for error whatsoever. If even the slightest thing went wrong, you would either explode, get eaten, or gag on what a million Chinamen ate last week, and if it was your lucky day, you'd get all three. You can imagine the relaxing effect this had on one, as one came in to land on a big bird.

And even *that* was nothing. Just more background. 'Final approach' was what gave you the *actual heart attack*, pretty much *every time.* Not for you the slow and stately descent, gradually getting closer and closer, lower and lower, until wheels kiss concrete with reassuring exactitude and maybe a wee bump. Not here, Baby. The old airport was surrounded by steep mountains, all of them bristling with residential skyscrapers packed to the gills with a very nervous middle-class, every family unit of which was expecting an extra couple of hundred guests, *flambé,* to drop in at any moment. You came in *around a mountain* packed with high-rises full of terrified Chinese, your huge wings pitched over at *appalling angles* all the way around, as the pilot was forced to *slalom* this colossal lump of ironmongery one way then the other to line it up wth the runway, *more or less!* At some point you would be keeled over so far that you would be convinced that this time, surely this time something *must be terribly wrong,* oh, this time *we must be going down!* You prayed for the plane to level out. But then the great beast would suddenly heel *all the way over onto its side,* wings pointing practically up and down, engines all screaming, some of the passengers screaming, everybody clutching at their armrests, as the pilot took his one very last chance at correction. Then, to really loosen your bowels, he would suddenly drop the nose into a swan-dive to fit the machine onto that little strip of tar. Some times it would feel like you were headed *straight into the ground.* Holy flammable Jesus! This is it, Baby!

At the last possible *second*, it seemed, he yanked on the stick and leveled her out so that the great firework didn't pogo along the runway, straight into a gas tanker with *your name* on it. You stare out the window to get the best possible view of the coming fireball, and… what the…? *There they are!* The slum apartments! They're whizzing by at eye level. You are among them! *You've practically moved in!* You feel you could reach out and slap five with the old geezers in their undies, smoking cheroots on the fire-escapes. It crosses your mind how unlikely it is that any of these people have ever felt the need of a laxative.

BANG! You hit the deck like a carrier-landing, and *roooaaaaaahh*, the retro-rockets slam on so hard your eyeballs protrude, every one of you in your own language inwardly mumbling the same mantra; "Please don't go in the water. Please don't go in the water. Please don't go in the water."

*Bing-Bong! "Welcome to Hong Kong, ladies and gentlemen. Maternity nurses are waiting at Arrivals to assist those ladies **or gentlemen** who may find that they have given birth. Adult diapers can be found next to the toilets at the Self-Soiling Station. Thank you and have a nice day,"*

So it was right after a particularly *bad* one of these hayrides that I was taking the courtesy-bus for the short hop into old Kowloon. Normally this would have been a pleasantly de-pressurizing jaunt, but no. On this particular trip I was painfully squished up against a vastly obese fellow-passenger, shoe-horned into a sliver of seat next to what I will charitably describe as a *hellacious porker.* I couldn't move. I could barely even breathe. Apropos of nothing at all, and without having previously said so much as hello, he suddenly turned to me and said, in a loud, very high-pitched American twang,

- I like your thighs.

It took me a moment to grasp what he had said. Squeezed up next to him like that, I barely had *room* to be shocked.

- I beg your pardon?

- I said I like your thighs.

- Ha ha.

- No, seriously. I really like 'em.

I stared straight ahead and said nothing. What could one *possibly add?*
Was this code? Had I been mistaken for a freemason? Was this a heart-
breaking example of Tourette's? Or was I - God forbid - actually being
hit on by this gigantic lard ass? Whichever it was, I didn't want to say
anything to provoke him further. I was jammed so tightly up against
him that there was nothing I could do if he turned nasty. He didn't even
need to whip out a weapon. If he just took a deep breath, all my internal
organs would rupture simultaneously. To crowbar my corpse out of
there would require large men and a large tub of butter.

- Your nips are nice, too.

- Oh my god. *Excuse* me?

- Your nips. Very nice.

- What?

- But your thighs... I really like.

- Oh, god.

- Ah, yeah, your thighs are... there's just something *about 'em,* know
  what I mean?

- No. No. I don't.

Now, let's get this straight. I don't object to being propositioned,
even if it is all a bit sudden and by a vast hog of the same sex. Live and
let live, I say. But this was clearly no idle flirtation. This was a blatant
list of specific body parts that had taken his fancy - my thighs and
nipples, to be exact. And it wasn't even that *that* was really bothering
me. It was the slobbering gaze and the morbid possibility that maybe
he wasn't thinking about them in *that way* at all. Maybe the fat bastard
was thinking of them more *in the way of a snack!*

- So!

- S-s-so?

- So! What do *you* think?

- About what?

- About your thighs?

- ????

- Have you been there before? Know what I mean?

- No, I don't know what you mean.

- Have you *been* there?

- Where?

- *You* know. To *Thigh*-land.

- *What?*

- Well, I assumed that since we were both flyin' in from *Bangkok*....
from *Thigh-land*...

- Oooooooh!

- Riiiiiiight.

- Oh, you mean Thailand!

- Yeah, Thailand, Thigh-land, however the hell you wanna say it.

- Oh, I *see*. So you mean you like *Thais*. The Thai *people*.

- Yeah. I *love* your Thighs.

- And... and... the *Japanese people,* too.

- Yeah. Your Nips. I like your Nips, too. But your Thighs I just *love*.

- Me too.

- Good. That's settled then.

So! Holy shit! Phew! Thank God. He wasn't nuts at all, just a moron. What a relief. I exhaled - a dangerous thing to do in the circumstances, especially when he suddenly whipped his head around and started in on me again, but this time with a kind of earnest, conspiratorial kind of stage whisper. Well, this was an *American* tourist. The closest any American tourist ever gets to a whisper could keep ships off the Grand Banks in a fog. Why *are* they so friggin' loud? Are they *weaned* too early?

- But I *will* tell ya somethin' for nothin', buddy.

- Oh?

- I'll tell you what I do *not* get.

- What?

- All this frickin' guff about regularity.

- Regularity?
- Damn right.
- What guff?
- Oh, come on, Buddy. You know what I'm talking about.
- No. I don't. Really.
- Sure you do.
- I don't.
- Don't give me that. Everybody's talkin' all this self-righteous hoo-ha about regularity. Like you don't know.
- I don't. I don't.
- Oh, sure you do. I just don't get what the big deal is. It drives me frickin' *crazy.*

Crazy? Bad choice of word, fat boy. Suddenly, I'm right back where I started. Visions of exploding spleens crowd the screen. How far is it to Downtown? Just get me to the ferry before this guy's medication wears off. The thighs and nipples thing was just a coincidence. But regularity? What the hell is he going on about? All I know is I'm pinioned next to a *regular* whack-job.

- Regularity, Buddy. They all act like it's the frickin' Holy Grail.
- They do?
- You know goddam well what I'm talkin' about. Bein' regular.
- What?
- You know. Goin'! Like... *goin'!*
- Going?
- To the *bathroom!*
- Ooohhh…
- Shittin' every day, fer Chrissakes.
- Oooooooohhh...
- Pinchin' off a frickin' *loaf* every morning. Droppin' a *log...*
- OK. OK, I get it. I get it. Regularity.
- Regu - frickin'- *larity!*
- OK. Regularity. What about it?
- That's all you frickin' hear these days. All this guff about you gotta

take a frickin' *dump* every morning. Like, every single *day?* Are they kiddin' me? Who shits every day? You know who shits every day? I'll tell you who shits every day. Nobody. That's who. *Nobody!*
Slowly I try to slide down between him and the armrest, to make myself less of a target in the event he should suddenly go *entirely* postal. But it's impossible to move. I'm stuck. I'll just have wait him out. I'll humor him. I'll engage him in conversation, yes, that's what I'll do.
- So. Er…
- Eric.
- So, Eric, how often do you, er… you know… *go?*
- Go? Me? Oh, the normal, I guess.
- And the normal would be…?
- About once a week.
- Really? So often?
- See! You're right! Yeah. It's more like once every two weeks.
- And you feel…OK.
- My point *exactly.* I feel great. Nothin' wrong with *me* is there?
- Nothing at all, Eric.
- Do I seem sick to *you?*
- Certainly not.
- Hah! See! Regularity my ass!

His ass? Another bad choice of image. Now all I can think about is his ass and what it is currently holding back *with difficulty.* The burning question is, of course, how long has it been since he took his last bi-weekly avalanche? Are we talking the entire fortnight here? Is he a big shit bomb ready to go off? Don't tell me there's a full two weeks' worth backed up in that hopper! How much can be contained by one poor, straining sphincter? This guy goes four hundred pounds, easy. What hideous tsunami is waiting in the offing, so to speak? Will he blow at any second? We are on a dangerously bumpy road, I notice. It occurs to me that of all the many possible ways I might shuffle off this mortal coil, this is not one that had previously presented itself: buried alive under an alp of turd.

The bus came to a merciful halt on the waterfront, where the merchant fleet was bracing itself for the next airliner, and there across the darkening bay, reflected in the water like wildfire was the blazing skyline of Hong Kong Island, lit up in the twilight like a billion juke-boxes against dark blue velvet. Visible from space. Fabulous. As ever. Big Eric bobbled off the bus directly ahead of me, careening dangerously off the seats like a big Macy's balloon full of shit. Once off the bus and on the ground, he turned around and extended his plump fingers for me to shake. I tried not to squeeze them *too* hard. You never know.

- Nice talkin' to ya, Buddy.
- Very nice, Eric.
- Say, is there a bathroom around here somewheres?
- Don't know. Sorry.
- Oh, well. I'll be headin' off this way, then. See what I can scare up.
- OK.
- 'Bye.

And off he wobbled. Scare up? Another brilliant choice. Off he went, lolloping along in search of whatever woefully inadequate receptacle he might terrify. It occurred to me that this was something the city fathers had never thought to plan for. Oh sure, they had a main sewer here that you could drive trucks through. I'd seen a photograph of it. But they hadn't met Eric. I walked away quickly in the opposite direction towards the ferry. I figured I should head to Hong Kong Island and out of poor old Kowloon while it was still dry land.

THE DOG ON THE BEACH

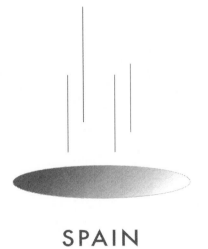

SPAIN

The dog on the beach was the last straw. In fact, whenever the phrase 'the last straw' is called for in normal conversation, I often find myself saying "Well, if that isn't just *the dog on the beach!*" But don't get me going on this.

The beach, of the dog on the beach, was near Tarragona, somewhere down there on the Spanish coast. It was on a long stretch of road that swoops dramatically up and down the hills, all very cinematic and historic. For miles, there seems to be a ruined castle on the top of every promontory overlooking the sea, reminding you that Spain was once the undisputed world champ of empire and sent armadas off to 'discover' far-flung parts of the world that had clearly been discovered already and had been in use quite publicly, for millennia, but what the heck. They had to be plundered anyway and burnt to the ground, for Christ's sake. Literally. Christ was on the side of Spain, you see, although he'd been dead for quite a while and probably had never heard of Spain. Or Christianity, for that matter. A minor quibble. So it was all perfectly kosher. Had to be done. Slaughter the lot of 'em, steal their gold, melt it down, bring it home, spend it. Hey, what would you rather have, a filigreed chalice of hand-spun gold that took a dozen Inca craftsmen a year to create? Or a turd-size lump of bullion that could rent you hairy-assed Spanish whores every night for the rest of your life back home in Madrid? No contest.

It was a glorious era for the manly art of genocide all around. And the Incas and Aztecs could hardly complain. They were slaughtering virgins just to see the looks on their faces. Oh, there are more elaborate explanations, of course, but the hieroglyphs are probably all bullshit. Ask the virgins.

So, as I rumbled along in the back of a truck, I was swelling with pride at the superb cruelty of my fellow man. I was hitch-hiking down to Almeria - a sweltering desert hole, where Italian movie makers were shooting American cowboy flicks. Spaghetti Westerns, they were calling them. This was the early 70s. It was a fabulous new era in the history of B-cinema and I intended to ride horses for a fistful of dollars. I wanted to be a pretend cowboy, like Clint Eastwood. True, I had never been anywhere near a horse, but I had ridden a tricycle as a child. And anyway I was desperate. After recently graduating from a great university with an honors degree in English, I was unemployable. But I could spell.

I began this wild horse chase pessimistically enough, with almost no money and full of remorse at having begun my adult life in such dire straits. And the further South I pilgrimmed, the deeper I sank into the Slough of Despond. By the time I hit Tarragona I was ready to slit my wrists. The truck ride terminated at an empty, windy saloon bar on the shore, where I spent my very last coins on several beers. Then I picked up my bag and stumbled tipsily down onto the bleak expanse of brown mud they were calling The Beach. It looked like the abandoned movie set of *Waiting For Godot*.

Dark clouds were lowering. Rain was imminent. The sun was going down in a very dramatic fashion, so the shit brown of the wet mud was flecked with red. It looked like either The Apocalypse, or an advanced bowel condition. I had no shelter and no sleeping bag. I was hungry and miserable. I set my little bag down and opened it up, looking through it for the something to eat that I knew was not there. I left it sitting with the top gaping wide open like a silent scream, like that horse in *Guernica*. I sat down and put my head in my hands. I may have seen a sadder day in my very young life, but at that moment I could not recall it. It was a real violin moment. I sat there for a long time with my chin on my knees and just stared blankly out to sea, cursing my stupid plan and my stupid life thus far.

But as my eyes scanned the grim horizon, aimlessly, they were occasionally taken with a small dot in the far distance, off to one side. It seemed to be moving slightly. I paid no attention to it at first, thinking I was either slightly drunk or so hungry my eyes were playing tricks. But soon all my attention was riveted on the meandering dot. It was something to look at. When young men are hit with horrible epiphanies about what total losers they are and how they have No Future, they will obsess on anything. A smudge on the ceiling. A fingernail. A dot. With my knees drawn up to my chin I sat there and stared at it. Was it a boat rocking far away? A buoy? A fisherman, perhaps? The beach was vast, the very low tide having pulled the sea out really far, and the dot was way out there at the water's edge, too far for me to make it out clearly, but I began to think it was getting slightly bigger. Then I realized that it *was* getting bigger and that whatever it was, it was coming in my direction.

After about fifteen more minutes of staring, I could see that it was a dog. And from the way it was moving it looked like a very old dog or a very gimpy one, or both. But it was a dog all the same, another sentient being. I was not alone in this Goya movie. Oh joy. And after a further long while watching it, I could not help but realize that out of this entire stretch of abject nothingness, the dog had apparently developed a similar fixation on me. It was mutual. There could be no doubt that it was wobbling and hobbling, limping and lolloping, slowly, ineluctably and, I fancied, *existentially...* towards me.

Ah, man's best friend, the noble dog, maybe not as precious as a wife, but far more accommodating, the proof being, to quote the old saying, that if you bring another woman home, a dog will happily play with *both* of you. A wife will not do that.

Ah, yes, and here he came a-wagging, my new old pal, my four-legged friend and companion in grief. Rover. There was light at the end of the tunnel. Rover *was* the light at the end of the tunnel. Good boy!

It never takes much, does it? Just a glimmer and we're back from the abyss. I felt quite bucked up. I started remembering some of the truly bizarre adventures I'd already had on this long, strange trip. Suddenly they didn't seem so bad on reflection, even fun, almost, in retrospect, especially the most shocking one of them all.

I had been standing for hours with my thumb out, bored shitless, on the side of the road outside of Vittoria, in the Basque country, on the exit ramp of a freeway (and remember, never put all your Basques in one exit. Ahem.) After several oven-baked hours of roasted uneventfulness, already deep in the bag of youthful melancholy and regret, a miracle happened. A bright white Renault Alpine with Paris plates, one of the coolest, fastest sports coupes ever built, screeched to a halt beside me with its engine screaming - *vroom! vrooooom!* - and the radio blasting. The driver leaned over with a maniacal grin, saying the magic French word, unheard in these parts all morning, *"Montez!"* Get in.

I got in. He floored it. We went from zero to a hundred in minus one second. I was thrown back in my seat, my face plastered against my skull, and in a heartbeat we were going faster than I had ever been in my life, on land, and I went from utter boredom to abject terror in the same minus-one-second interval. The maniac was yelling *Yeeeeeeeaaah!* as we went roaring through village after village, scattering dogs, ducks, chickens and terrified peasants to either side of us. I had been delivered from total tedium into the hands of a raving lunatic. The slight pang of panic at being a loser at twenty-one was replaced by the awful possibility that I would never see the age of twenty-two.

He *whooped* as we flew, cheering every near-miss and near-vehicular-homicide. I whooped, too, getting into the spirit of the thing, whatever the hell *the thing* was, but I don't think I stopped inwardly muttering omigod, omigod, omigod until we screeched to a halt in a cloud of dust, fifty or so miles down the road, in the parking lot of a fancy restaurant somewhere, I don't know where, as the sun was going down and some Mariachi-type band was playing picturesquely in the local square at this golden hour, everything dappled in gilded light. It was a heavenly scene, especially as it followed near-death.

What the car radio had been blaring was a breathless blow-by-blow report of the Le Mans 24-hour race which was taking place at that very moment across the border in France, and what had whipped this whack-job into such a frenzy was the fact that an identical Renault Alpine, just like his but with a number on the side, was currently zooming around the Le Mans track, in this same golden twilight, leading its engine-class and kicking some serious automotive ass over there in Parley-Vous. You would think that this crazy sonofabitch had actually designed, built and driven the damned car himself, the way he was carrying on. Every time the heroic Alpine was mentioned in the commentary, he whooped louder and his foot went down further and shoved another ten mph through the tail-pipe. How we had arrived here in one piece, only God knew, and he was probably watching it through his fingers.

But every car-mad Basque kid on the street had apparently been following every detail of the big race on the radio, too, and as we climbed out of the suddenly-famous vehicle, we were mobbed by a pack of them, all howling in youthful, automaniacal admiration, back-slapping and cheering us. We were escorted into the restaurant like rock stars by the picturesque little snot-noses and, as we were about to go in, Nutcase turned around to them and made some sort of show-off speech to big cheers all around, and actually signed a few autographs. There's no prick like a rich prick. This is a known fact.

He made no secret of already being pretty shit-face drunk when we sat down, but that didn't stop him from ordering a bottle of excellent wine, then an even better one and several superfine VSOP brandies, as we tucked into the signature dish of this fancy joint, famous far and wide for this one item - squid cooked in its own ink. It was as black as anthracite. It was like slurping a can of lumpy paint. I wondered what my nice pink insides were looking like, round about now.

When we finally exited, the night was as black as the soup and we were both drunk as skunks. We actually had to hold onto each other to remain upright. But, having had a head start, the driver was even more legless than I was and I remember thinking, as I *helped him* into his driver's seat, he being unable to manage it alone, 'Should I really be, you know, *getting back in* to this six-speed coffin? Is this not, basically, *suicide?*' But then I remembered that I *was* suicidal. Duh. I had totally forgotten in all the excitement. Thank God I remembered. So I got back into the projectile and off we roared, possibly even faster than before, my man having lost every last shred of caution or, come to think of it, every last shred of the subtler motor functions or of *full consciousness.*

Fortunately it was nighttime, and on the freeway that runs due South over the empty high-desert moonscape between the Basque country and Madrid, the road was new and perfect, and perfectly empty. We didn't see another car coming or going the whole way, so we were alone on a superfast superhighway. What harm could befall? There was nothing to hit. So I began to relax, despite the insane speeds we were achieving, the radio reports still urging our loony on to vicarious glory as the Le Mans 24-hour race zoomed into the neighboring night, across the border.

But then I began to feel the first rumblings in my stomach as the too-much wine began to argue with the too-much brandy. It started out as a civil enough disagreement, but degenerated fast into an ugly brawl. I was pretty sure the whole shit-fight was about to come roaring out and redecorate the car's hand-tooled interior. Oh dear. 'Do you mind *eef* I open the *ween*-dow, for a *leetle beet* of fresh air?" I asked in my excellent Spanish. *'Yeeeeeeeaah!!!'* replied the bug-eyed whack-job. I took this for permission. I rolled down the window and the rush of cold, dark air proved to be the clinching argument in the court-case going on down below. I barely managed to jam my head out in time for the big black firework to go off into the night. And then again. And again. And again. When I had hurled what felt like everything north of my asshole, I slid my head back inside and cast a baleful eye over towards him. He hadn't noticed. The roar of the wind had silenced the whole horrendous *aria.* Thank heavens. The meal had been exorbitantly expensive and I had just tossed it. One hates to appear unappreciative.

It also hit me that since we were going at light speed down a wind tunnel, the inky black upchuck might also have been brushed back a wee bit by the gale, thereby slightly freckling his pristine paintwork. This was, after all, a meticulously maintained vehicle in twinkling shiny white. So I stuck my head out again and looked back along the side of the impeccably clean machine, for traces of the odd stray fleck.

I looked. I saw. Oh, sweet regurgitating Jesus! *Say it ain't so!*

The entire side of the car was plastered an inch deep in sticky black squid sick, like one of those flame patterns on the side of a hot-rod, but this one utterly disgusting. From the front window all the way back, an ever-widening holocaust of black hurl fanned out until around the tail lights it was floor to roof like fresh-laid road tar drying to a vile crust in the night air. The car had been white. It was now white with a black puke triangle. Well, *it's a look*, I thought.

I made plans to exit the vehicle quickly when the time came, and to dash around to the driver's side to bid goodbye to Nutcase, because who knew what he might do if he were to see how I had turned his clean machine into a sonnet to vomit. He was the big, muscular, no-neck type of loony, too. He could easily have torn my heart out and scraped the black muck off with *that*, if provoked. I would just insist that he didn't get out to shake hands. Yes. That should do it. Come to think of it, he was *incapable* of getting out, So I began to relax. Again. And I started to feel way better all around, as one generally does after the horror of being violently turned inside out.

I scrunched back into my customized black leather bucket seat and just enjoyed the high-speed show unfolding in the headlights in front of me like a 3D video game. Wow. Hurtling into the night at warp speed on a brand new asphalt surface, surreally smooth, a long tongue of black, unfurling ahead, mostly dead straight, with sharp, bright new lines recently painted on it, white for the lanes and yellow for the edge that marked the soft shoulder of ochre dirt in this bone dry, empty, featureless high desert, with us tearing towards Madrid on it, all alone. It was totally empty, adding to the unreality. Not one car. Nothing. Ever. In either direction, for mile on mile.

And this was a *real* sports car, not a souped-up coupe with a stripe. Low-slung, mere inches above the black macadam, our legs out straight ahead and the driver's seat pushed all the way back so that his arms were out straight like a race driver's and we were clearly flying as fast as she would fly, way, *way* over a hundred mph for mile on mile on mile, a starfighter zooming into black infinity. Wow. What a feeling.

Then it happened, sudden, fast and terrifying.

A thrilling, long left bend unwound in front of us. The road was banked way up on the right hand side so that drivers could take the corner at full speed. Which we did. And which we should not have done. The steeply raked curve had been designed for fast cars, yes, but not for a supercharged Renault Alpine being gunned foot-to-the-floor by a reckless, drunken dingbat at damn near a hundred and a half. We squealed across *all* the white lines to the yellow line on my side of the road. He couldn't hold it. We crossed the line, hit the dirt hard and... Voop! We went airborne.

Airborne. Airborne. Aiiiiirboooooorne. For looooong seconds. End over end in the air, engine screaming, car rotating, ass over tit until.... *BOOOOF!* we hit the deck upside down, rear-end-first and *wheeeeee!!...* aiiiiiiiirboooorne again... end over end and *BOOOOF!* ...flipped over one more time and *BAM!...* landed upside down and spun a few times on the roof, and then *Crack!,* the long, sloping rear window popped out as we skidded along, tits up in the sagebrush, the sharp gorse and cactus of the desert being scooped into the car all around our heads until we ...*BUMP!* stopped dead against a low rill of hard sand.

Sweet road-wrecking Jesus! We're alive. I've banged my head and elbow and wrist a few times, but I'm OK, upside down, gasoline pouring from the upended vehicle into the car roof, which is now the floor. Nut-Job has the presence of mind to turn off the *squealing, roaring engine.* 'You OK?' 'Yes.' 'You OK?' 'Yes. Get out, get out, *get out! It's going to exploooooode!!!*

The popped-out long rear window-hole gave us easy egress as we

THE DOG ON THE BEACH

snaked and wriggled on our backs through the stony sand and among the desert plants, birthing ourselves side by side through it, me grabbing my small bag on the way, and both of us limping into the dark away from the imminent explosion, tripping over tussocks and roots till we were at a safe distance, then turning round and looking at the total catastrophe we had just escaped from miraculously, both of us virtually unmarked, just dirtied and bloodied. God takes care of drunks. This is also a known fact.

My bag was flattened. Luckily there were only clothes in it. I fished in it for my soft pack of Spanish cigarettes. It was unrecognizable, squished to the thickness of a crepe. I kept it for years afterwards as a souvenir, a reminder of how that flattened ciggy pack had almost been my head. The insane luck of walking away from such a spectacular car wreck is incalculable. The car was way beyond totaled. The engine block may have been salvageable, but nothing else. It had been arguably one of the prettiest small sports cars ever built, this one cared for and shiny as a new dime. It had been low to the ground but it was now *below* ground, flattened out into an unrecognizable mash of shattered metal and paint. And vomit. It looked like an egg-white omelet with black seafood accents.

The weirdest thing was that we were suddenly surrounded by people and cops, we who had been alone on the road for hours. A truck full of workers and security guys had joined the expressway from a nearby side path and had lit us up in their headlight just as we were about to execute our aerial ballet. They could not believe what they had just witnessed. Nobody said much. The totality of destruction stunned them all into silence. They simply could not credit that we had walked away, and they kept asking us if we were OK. But Whacko's noisy non-stop sobbing was merely over the loss of his expensive penis extension, not about anything serious. The prick had merely lost an inch or two off his prick.

I spent that night in an abandoned car the cops pointed out to me when they drove us both into the silent, empty Madrid city center

217

in the dead of night, along with the workers. A perfect bed for a broke young hitchhiker. I'd asked for a cell, but they'd said no. I slept like the corpse I so nearly had been. I woke up to a blinding sun boiling my hung-over brain in the oven of the old jalopy and discovered that the car was on a traffic island in the busiest intersection in Madrid at peak morning rush hour. It took me half an hour to cross the road, dehydrated, still drunk, and feeling like hammered dogshit. But in one piece. The quest would continue, towards the kind of great wages I'd heard you could earn as a pretend cowboy just like Clint Eastwood, in Almeria, still far off to the South. And that was only two days ago.

Now this. The empty beach. Still so far to go and literally without a penny. But, hey, at least I was not alone. Rover the dear old dog was ambling closer, doggedly.

I became suddenly quite teary-eyed, but in a warm and fuzzy way, reflecting on the warm-and-fuzzy relationship we have with these affectionate, sweet-natured, soulful beasts who live right alongside us but on another planet, in a miasma of sensory semiotics we have no access to, no concept of, and yet who so easily bridge that gap that they act as if incomplete without their joined-at-the-heart pet human. How easily we are all moved to tears by any talk about the love and loyalty and near worship they pour out so unstintingly to even the meanest and most undeserving assholes among us, content simply that we are there, intuiting our various shades of sad, from the blues to the darkest despair, and by just waddling over to lick our hand or to just look up at us with that comically hang-dog stare of untutored, unfiltered and unlimited sympathy, they break the spell, get a grudging smile out of us, make us put away the gun.

Just like old Rover here, standing unsteadily in front of me, swaying from his huge effort, panting hard from his long trek of companionship and his tongue damn near touching the ground, the old fleabag, manfully, dogfully, trying to wag his old tail, having hobbled and stumbled up the last few steep yards of incline to lick my hand, or show some other sign of doggy affection. He's broken the spell. Saved my life. And half killed himself doing it. How can I be so down when there is such simple, pure love wafting around in the world? All you need is love. Isn't that so, eh, old fella? Come on over here and let me give your ear a scratch and hope I don't get your fleas.

He limps over the last few feet, my only friend, my hairy old savior. I put out my palm out for him to lick. He stops. He sniffs it. He raises his big old head. He has a good look at me. He doesn't lick. He turns slightly and walks right past me up the same sandy path that I came down on my way from the road. He passes my bag that is still standing there forlornly with its mouth wide open like a silent scream, like that horse in *Guernica*. He stops and looks at it. And then he... he *what?* He WHAAAAT?!

He lifts his leg and *PISSES IN IT?* A perfect aim! A big fat stream of steaming stinky dog piss!! Right into the wide open mouth of my *only bag* with all of my *only clothes* and my *only* towel and toothbrush and.... I start screaming! *You FUCKAAAAHHH!!!*

I try to jump up, but I fall over my own feet which have gone to sleep, so long have I been squatting there on my haunches waxing so philosophical about this... stupid.... pissing *piece of SHIT.* I'm flailing around trying to get upright, while he's *still pissing!* He's not paying the damnedest bit of attention to me rolling around in the dirt, screaming at him, trying to stand up. The rotten bastard is just *pissing away!* He's ruining everything in there, everything I have in the world, my only chance of making it the next few hundred miles to work and to money and to *Clint FUCKING EASTWOOD!*

You FUCKAAAHHH!!! You... FUCKAAAAHHH!!!

I grab a rock big enough to kill the bastard and I hurl it from a sitting position and it goes sailing right past his ear and he just *keeps on pissing!* He hasn't even *noticed?* How fucking stupid can you be, *you fucking... FUCKAAAHHH!!!?*

I'm homicidal... *doggicidal!* I'm ready to kick the living shit out of him. And he's just standing there looking at me like a.... but my feet suddenly come back into circulation and I stand up and scream some yodeling banshee curses at him, take a deep breath and just *launch* myself at him at full tilt and aim a huge, murderous kick at his big thick head. But he jumps back! I miss hugely and go flying sideways into my own *disgusting, stinking, piss-soaked wide-open bag*!

Aaaaaaaarrrrghhhh!!!! motherFUCKAAAHHH!!!

And he *finally* gets it. 'Uh-oh. I'm in trouble.' And he's off. He's loping off up the path to the road as I'm scrambling to my slightly drunken feet and bounding over my filthy, disgusting, piss-filled bag and screaming at him and chasing him up towards the road as fast as I can. I want to *kill* him. I want to take him down like a rugby tackler and twist his *stupid fucking head off* and smash his stupid fucking skull *with a fucking rock* and I wanna... I wanna... I wanna...

I wanna say... I *gotta* say... as I come reeling to the top of the rise, panting for breath, and watch him legging it off along the side of the road at full tilt, ears flat against his big head, I gotta say, yes... *I gotta...* hand it to him.

Yes. I gotta hand it to him. That crippled old cocksucker can *run*.

THE BOYS NEXT DOOR

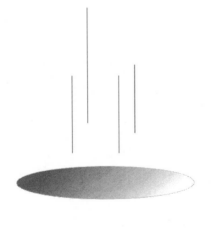

NEW YORK

The crazy 80s in New York City were just about to kick off when this all happened. It started in that blank period between Christmas and New Year. It's a strange time. A friend once likened it to that little speed bump between the vagina and the anus - neither one thing nor the other, but still oddly festive.

It's also a time for reflection and I was reflecting - the sun setting on one thing and dawning on another thing, sort of thing. This might also have been because, through a bullet-hole in my bathroom window, I could see one of those stunning New York sunsets that make you thank God... that New Jersey is so polluted.

I was in one of the cheapest and vilest hotels in Manhattan. This was years ago when there were scores of dumps like it all over the island, but this one was arguably the winner. It was called The Earle - or The Oil, as it was pronounced by the ex-con who answered the phone. I was living there because I was broke, so I was not in the best of spirits to begin with, and this weird interim season didn't help. The joyful sound of Christmas carols and the happy tinkling of Santa's bell have always made me want to kick an elf in the nuts at the best of times. But this particular season of mirth was made even fouler by the fact that the two guys who shared the hotel room next to mine were apparently having the time of their lives. They were almost expiring with joy on a daily basis. Through the very thin walls, all I heard for weeks, night and day, was laughter and chuckling and the occasional fit of hysterics. It was sickening.

And here they were, at it again this early winter's eve, chortling and sniggering away through the papery wall as I sat there straining on my lonesome toilet and the sun went down in a glorious, petrochemical farewell to another miserable day in this shit hole of a hotel.

The Earle was a world-class hovel. A few days earlier there had been some talk of a dead junky being found in the elevator and nobody seemed surprised. Junkies, dealers and hookers made up most of the establishment's roster - and musicians, of course. But then, some of the musicians were also dealers, several were whores and all of them were junkies, so that item didn't really add anyone to the list. Fortunately the musicians were mostly punk rockers with chunks of metal sticking out of their heads by way of jewelry, so - since none of them could play a lick or cared to learn one - we were at least spared the noise of practice.

It was bitterly cold too, that winter. It had been a white Christmas, so the entire city was still under its romantic coverlet of slush and dog shit. The pooper-scooper law had not yet been passed, so Manhattan looked as it did every winter, as if it were covered in Rocky Road ice cream, but you wouldn't want to lick it. There was so much dog shit lying around in those days that you would find yourself prancing around like Fred Astaire just to get down the street unscathed. Everybody had a dog then. New York was dangerous in those days. You *needed* a dog to bark at the drug addicts who pushed your door in and waved a gun in your face, and then you needed it to bark at them again on their way out as they lurched off under the weight of your TV. One feels almost wistful at the memory of such sincere rudeness now that Manhattan has begun to toy with the idea of civility.

God, it was cold. The Earle banged and hissed with radiators night and day and stank of their sticky drool - although I was told that in summer it stank even worse without their help. The walls were so thin they were mostly just paint, which had the effect of turning them into diaphragms, amplifying the next-door sounds they were supposed to muffle. So there was no avoiding the racket one neighbor could inflict on another. It was a flimsy dump all around. If the cockroaches hadn't all been holding hands, the whole frigging place would have fallen down.

But the Earle's legendary status in the annals of filth had coincided with the Punk fad, so the place had acquired a certain seedy swagger. The clientele was fashionably hideous, colorful in a bad-teeth sort of way. The nearby Chelsea Hotel was the place to be, of course, for that pleasant veneer of bohemian crud. The Earle was neither pleasant nor bohemian and the crud was no veneer, but it was half the price of the Chelsea so we thought we were twice as cool. We were pathetic.

When he handed me my key on the night I showed up with my suitcase full of crap and my shoes full of iced turd, the night clerk, another jailbird, said, "You got the best room in the joint, kid. You got the only one wit' a balcony." I felt quite cheered up until I saw the balcony. It was two feet square. It was also two feet deep in pigeon shit, and the window was painted shut anyway, so you couldn't get out there even if you did hanker after the thrill of standing up to your knees in a cube of avian dung.

The paint in my room was a bilious yellow with brown stencils that were meant to be flowers, but what it actually looked like was dried piss flecked with diarrhea. I fell on the bed with a Wagnerian groan, and decided that my life had hit bottom. Then the beamish boys next door started up and I realized there was still a long way down to go.

And here I still was, weeks later, athwart the can at sunset, moaning in the gloaming, the very fact that I was squatting here at this hour proof enough that not one thing in my life was on schedule. And to add insult to irregularity, my vigil was accompanied by the loud fraternal ecstasy of the boys adjacent. I decided then and there that enough was enough. I would simply have to confront the bastards. I had never actually seen either of them, but I had a pretty clear picture. They were obviously two very different types. One sounded big, with a deep voice. All you heard from him was a rumble of comment. He never laughed much. He just made the *other* guy laugh. And it was *this* son of a bitch I wanted to eviscerate.

He had a high-pitched little squeak like a chihuahua and he was such a cheap laugh that anything could set him off. And the big guy clearly knew how to tickle him. So he was constantly either tittering at a rumbled remark or squealing at the occasional zinger. And in between those extremes he went through the entire gamut of chuckles, sniggers, chortles, giggles, twitters, whoops, yelps, honks, shrieks, and for the really big occasion, something that sounded like a helium-sniffing masochist having multiple orgasms while being bludgeoned to death.

The sun went down over Jersey and my own belated comment on it fell eight floors to the Greenwich Village sewer. I jumped into the shower, washed, scrubbed, shampooed, flossed, brushed, and selected the least crumpled items from my limited wardrobe on the floor. At least everything matched. Everything was black - shirts, socks, shoes, jackets, pants, underwear, everything. Everybody wore black then. If you didn't, you were a social retard. For a few years back there it looked as if an entire generation of downtown Manhattan belonged to some funerary cult. So I exited my pigeon-shit balcony-suite in fashionable mourning as per fad, but before heading out on the nightly trawl, I took a deep breath, stopped in front of the neighbors' door, and pounded on it.

The racket inside stopped dead. There was silence all around. Well, there was silence except for the usual belching of the radiators and the usual faking of an orgasm by the whore down the hall ("Oh God! Oh Jesus! Oh God! Oh Jesus!"). So I banged again. There was a rustle of furtive whispering behind the thin wall to the effect of, "You go." "No. You go." "No, you.' "No. *Yoouuu.*" It went on for so long that I yelled out, "OK! Make up your *fucking minds!*" Silence again. Then the door opened very slowly. I was, shall we say, unprepared for what greeted me.

A shortish, fattish, baldish, youngish man stood there with a look that can only be described as sheepish. He had a snickering, high-pitched way about him. But his most remarkable feature was that he was wearing a very short red tee shirt that ended well above his navel. And that was it. There was nothing else. Nothing whatsoever. I looked straight at his cock.

Oh, shit. I yanked my eyes back up and tried to act like I hadn't looked straight at it. I fixed my eyes on the lintel over the doorway so that he couldn't possibly think I was checking it out. "Is it about the noise?" he twittered, in that squeaky little voice I had come to know and love. I muttered something about trying to keep the racket down in the future, if you don't mind. But I was now addressing my remarks to the cracks in the wall above the lintel, which was itself way above his head, so that he couldn't possibly get the wrong idea. He squeaked something to the effect that he was very sorry, and closed the door on me. I heard the two of them stage-whispering behind the door, "It's your fault." "No, it's not. It's you." "No. It's you." "No it's you." "No, it's *yoouuu.*"

I shot down all sixteen flights, scuttled along Washington Square past the dope dealers who *still* tried to sell me a dime bag despite the fact that I was technically *sprinting,* and ducked into Emilio's Bar. As the Maker's Mark slid down the inside of my neck I explained to Gus the bartender how, the next time the bailiffs banged on his door or the cops called out his name from the hallway, he should always remember to open the door with his cock out and they would just walk away. He listened to me with the smile he reserved for mental patients.

Drunk, stoned and later, I picked my way gingerly through the brown and yellow ice-cream sundae of lower Manhattan, occasionally pulling a quick Fred Astaire, until I made it, without compromising the suede, all the way to The Mudd Club, which was situated in that blank strip between SoHo and Chinatown, an odd spot, really, neither one thing nor the other, not unlike that little no-cigar zone between the pussy and the New Year.

The Mudd Club was the hottest club in downtown Manhattan in those days, a reputation partly due to the fact that it was the *only* club in downtown Manhattan. It was a bleak and godforsaken hole, perfect for a generation that spent hours dressing up to look bleak and godforsaken. It was a kind of heaven for the kind of people who looked like they might prefer hell. And hell was where the doorman told most people to go. He wouldn't let anybody in to socialize unless they looked sufficiently anti-social. And there was really nothing inside when you got in there but peeling paint. But then we wanted so little - just a quick drink in a dirty glass and a quick feel in a dirty toilet. It wasn't a club at all, really. It was a mating facility, where the studiously sullen could fondle the fashionably frayed. To music.

We were all pretty ragged-ass in those days. The concept of pursuing a career had not yet been revealed to us. For the likes of us, The Mudd Club was the center of our so-called lives. Since landing in town I had landed a job writing for the local SoHo paper. The pay was a joke but it gave me the usual cadging rights, so that although my living quarters may have been cheesy, I was persona *au gratin* in certain concentric circles, the Mudd Club being the bullseye. I didn't have to pay for anything, anywhere. As long as I went to every party and every opening, I could stay drunk, stoned and fed for free. My own area of so-called journalism was so-called music. I wrote about the kind of virtuosi who lived in The Earle and attempted intercourse in the Mudd Club toilet, while their ladylike consorts were bent over the porcelain, delicately snorting lines of white powder off the off-white plastic seat.

That, in a snapshot, was the 'downtown scene', to be frank. There were about seven people doing anything of interest, as usual. But we journalistic flim-flam artists encouraged the rumor that something epic was going on, some steaming welter of undiscovered genius, so that we could maintain our freebie lifestyle. And eventually, bit by bit, it really *did* happen. Kids with actual talent *did* start to flood into downtown Manhattan, looking for this pig-trough of creative juices we were touting in our breathless dispatches. So it eventually became everything we said it was. We were no different from that whore down the hall, really. We certainly had the same motto. Fake it, and they will come.

The club was a small place and dark, and while my eyes were still adjusting, I got knocked right off my feet by a big slab of meat who stepped right over me and kept on walking. I jumped up off the floor and grabbed one of his shoulders. He spun around and I was flabbergasted by what faced me. The bruiser who had just walked through me like a linebacker, was a woman. She pushed her red, bloated face right into mine and yelled over the very loud music, "Why *not*, eh? Why fucking *NOT*?" Then she turned on her flat heels and stumped up the stairs.

to the second floor. "Holy shit", somebody next to me said, "Who the fuck was *that* hag?"

The shock was that I knew exactly who that hag was. She had once been one of the most heavenly creatures anyone in this place could ever have fantasized about. Just a few years earlier, she had been fabulously, ridiculously beautiful. She had been a famous muse, a girlfriend of the English rock aristocracy, the most desirable creature in a world so hip that only dogs could hear it. One notorious nude scene in one notorious movie had the entire hipster elite lined up in serried ranks of penile salute from London to New York. There are probably dedicated film students out there right now, still studying that scene, one-handed, flipping back and forth, Rewind, Play, Rewind, Play, to ponder every last detail of that sylph-like silhouette with its Nordic nipples pointing up at the North Star. Now look at her - a slab of gristle with a temper.

How had this happened so fast? People get old, but this was different. This was Cinderella turning into an ugly sister. I felt oddly bereft. She had been one of my unattainable dreams, all sinuous angularity, slim fingered, long limbed and ethereal. Now she looked like a bricklayer in a frock.

She clomped up the stairs and I followed her in a kind of blank daze. Well, let's not get too carried away here. I was in a blank daze when I arrived. I spent most of my *time* in a blank daze, to be brutally honest. But you get the picture.

The little upstairs room was used as a VIP lounge, although a P didn't have to be VI to get in. Writing for the local rag was enough. Once inside I saw her right away because the room was almost empty and she was sitting at a small round table, alone, facing the door, and me. I walked over and sat across from her. She gave me a kind of shrug and a grunted apology and I bummed a cigarette from her, so we were square. But, anyway, all that knocking over and yelling business was immediately forgotten, because there was now something far more shocking than her changed appearance to occupy every last microwave of my attention. Between us, thrown casually onto the center of the table in a tall white heap, was about a pound of cocaine.

I had never seen anything so electrifying. I had never seen anything so indecent, so desirable, so expensive, so illegal, so sexy, so likely to make you lose your precious cool and start humping the furniture. I have still never seen anything quite like that one stark naked pound of twinkling, mind-blowing blow. And it just sat there. Neither of us mentioned it. She just smiled at me a hard, confrontational sort of smile. I gave her back my own lame attempt at the same. I was trying with great difficulty to look only at her, not at *it*. Actually, I was trying to do both things at once. I was attempting a very difficult feat: one eyeball pointing at her, one down at the coke. like those chameleons on National Geographic TV.

But it was impossible to stay cool. Forget it. And forget my years of sexual yearning for this fallen angel and the recent frisson of poignancy at the memory of her lost loveliness. If I could just divert this fat cow's attention for ten seconds and run out of here with this pound of coke in my pocket, I could pay my rent at the Earle for the *entire frigging year*. I could even pay a Mexican to shovel the shit off my balcony so that I could stand on it every Sunday afternoon in my underwear, like Mussolini, shouting encouragement to the pot dealers down below in Washington Square, busy selling small baggies of dried oregano to law students and future public prosecutors.

But how the hell could I pull this off? This wasn't like breaking somebody's glasses and stealing their lunch. This kind of score could land me in some kind of junky witness protection program. I had to calm down and think fast. When opportunity knocked you had to pay attention. And when opportunity not only knocked, but broke down your door, pulled down your pants and started blowing you, one had to pay *particular* attention. But one glance at that alp of toot, and I was more than just attentive, I was a coiled spring. I was on such a hair-trigger at this juncture that if somebody had merely touched me on the shoulder, I would have shot through that second storey window like a howitzer shell and bit people on the leg when I hit the sidewalk.

"Hey", she said.

What? What? Was she talking to me? I had to control myself and try to figure out what she was saying in that odd Germanic accent, because my brain was fully occupied with leaping over the table, knocking her out, shoveling the shit into my pocket, jumping through that window, swinging onto the next building, lasooing a street-lamp, hi-jacking a taxi...

"Hey", she said. "It's salt".

Salt? What's salt? Is that code? Is salt the new code for.. for...freebase? Oh my God it's a whole pound of *freebase?* I'm rich! I'll *buy* the fucking Earle Hotel. Yes, that's what I'll do. I'll buy it and then I'll rent it out only to models. No. Only to *Brazilian* models. Yessss! I'll have two-way mirrors everywhere. The entire joint will be a honeycomb of peepholes. I'll wank myself blind. I'm rich! I'm rich and I'm blind! Hooray!

- Hey. I'm serious, man. It's just salt.

- Salt? You mean... salt as in... pepper?

- Yeah. It's just salt.

- Er.... I *knew that.*

- You *did?*

- Yes. Of course. Salt. Ha ha.

- Isn't it funny?"

- *HYSTERICAL!*

- Just watching peoples' reaction when they think it's coke?

- Ha ha! Yes! I do that all the time.

- You should sit here with me for a while and just watch. It's a trip.

- Yes. Let's do that, shall we? Can I have another cigarette?

- You're still smoking the last one.

- So I am. Can I have another?

Fuck. Fuckfuckfuck! Left tit! Right tit! FUCK! *Salt? Just salt?*

But she was right. It *was* funny. Our mound of gleaming *faux*-caine became the eye of a comic hurricane. It's true what they say about a large pile of coke. Fake it, and they will come. And one by one and two by two, they came, all the *unusual* suspects. Pretty soon we were surrounded by Le Tout Downtown, or rather Le Toot, gathering around us in a knot of barely-contained hysteria disguised as nonchalance. It was like watching a pack of blood-crazed hyenas try to sneak up on a water buffalo by dancing *Swan Lake* on point. They weren't fooling anyone, but it was hilarious to watch.

There were no chairs except for our two, no reason whatever for anybody to be there, packing themselves like sardines around this empty table in this empty room as the word spread. There was no reason to be there at all but for the mountain of white powder. And yet, like us, nobody mentioned it. There was nary a peep re the old *objet*. God forbid that anyone should be so uncool. They just stood around this little table, all doing the National Geographic chameleon, one eye on each other, one on Charlie. They craned their necks like geese, they chattered like finches, eyes darting around the circle for clues, for hints, for any glimmer that they may be invited at some pre-arranged signal to ram their collective snout into that big twinkling tit of toot. But they were damned if they would mention it. No way, man. Coke? What coke?

Only one guy, some unemployed grave-robber with a dripping nose who was way past caring, was vulgar enough to lean into my shoulder and whisper, "Hey, man. Is that real?" I looked up at him and whispered back, "Is *what* real?"

It was a convocation of craving around a cathedral of answered prayer. Not one eye left that table for one second. The Empress Catherine of All The Russias could have been buggered by a Cossack's horse in the opposite corner, and nobody would have torn their *one eye* away from that obscene promise lying right there before God and everybody.

But - fine comedy of manners though was - my gaze kept drifting back to the woman across from me, Marley's Ghost, sitting there with those calcified features and a look as mirthless as a hardened artery, performing this cruel experiment on these wingless gadflies buzzing in circles around her. It didn't even look as if she was having any fun. It looked - strange as may sound - like revenge.

Aha! So here we were again in that ontological lacuna between the asshole and Christmas, that time of reflection between the end of one thing and the start of another. I kept glancing at the Grim Warning across from me with the kind of focus reserved for moments of home truth.

Was she the first glimpse of the stoned pigeons coming home to roost? My attitude to drugs up until then had been the same as everyone else's. They were only bad when they ran out. We could handle anything. Coke was a good thing, surely. It made really cute girls want to do you right now. Quaaludes? Democracy in pill form. They made *everybody* look doable. Speed? Well, what could be wrong with writing that novel in three days while re-painting the apartment and still having time to re-alphabetize your record collection? As long as you could resist the urge to *actually chew off your own tongue*, speed was health food, wasn't it? Morphine? Mmmm, like having your genitalia licked by a very large aspirin. Cigarettes = Oxygen. Booze = Liquid Oxygen. Pot? Be serious. Heroin? Well, see, we're only *sniffing* it here, and frankly I rather prefer myself when I'm a little less vivacious. Opium? OK, there was a problem with opium. You could never find any. A flippant attitude towards drugs? Us? Au contraire, motherfucker. We were all *deeply appreciative*.

Drugs were not stopping us from 'being all we could be'. We were all just on hold, life-wise, anyway. And it was fun on hold. There was good music on hold. Hold was a club like The Mudd Club where you never had to go home unless you were with a chick on coke who couldn't wait to jump you and who looked sensational because you'd just taken a Quaalude. Come to think of it, in those days nobody ever went to bed with an unattractive person. We just woke up with a few, that's all. But was it all coming to some kind of bitter end? Was there an actual *price* to pay? Was I *looking at it?*

I took one last glance at her, the spirit of Christmas Future, and went back downstairs to cadge a drink. I needed one. But the bar was mobbed by a different clump of undiscovered genius, all rubbernecking something at the bar. Suspecting a fiasco like the one upstairs, I nevertheless elbowed my way to the front, being a newly minted journalist and all. But unlike the one upstairs, this particular object of desire had a pulse, in fact it had pulses racing. Surrounded by her own buzz of static and leaning against the counter was a girl with one beautiful breast. Well, she did have two but one was big and pert and perfect. And it was naked.

The *blasé* were agog. It was not that they hadn't seen one before, just that they hadn't seen *only one* before. The entire left side of her little black dress above the waist was absent. It might have been designed for Lord Nelson's girlfriend, so that on entering Admiralty balls, the couple would look, you know, coordinated. It was just flat-out filthy, poking out there alone like some lewd wink. Some things should hunt in pairs, damn it. Ask Noah. It was the lactic equivalent of a limp - just plain unsettling. But it was magnificent, too, I must say. She was one healthy mammal, all right. The craning barflies were beside themselves, gamely trying to look bored, but clearly on the point of gang-nursing. She was posing languorously against the counter while being photographed by another pretty girl who was snapping away and fluttering around. I stood there for a moment like a deer caught in *one* headlight, wondering how to introduce myself. What suave gambit does The Press venture in such a circumstance? "Nice tit?"

I stepped forward anyway and whipped out my shiny new press pass, while executing an involuntary chameleon.

- SoHo Weekly!
- Oh, great!

There was a pause as I selected the most eloquent opening.

- Nice tit.
- Oh, *thank* you. So, you're into Body Art, too?
- Well, I know what I *like*. What's your name?
- Erin Sane. Well, that's not my real name. The Erin part is, but not the Sane. That's David Bowie. Like *Aladdin Sane?* God, I loved that album. And that title. Like, a lad insane? You know? I always thought that, like, if only *my* first name ended in "in," I would love to do that, too. And then one day, it just hit me that...it *did!*

While the Body Artist was busy recalling her Epiphany, the snapper and I were trading glances and I could now see that she was far prettier than I had thought, her own charms having been so dimmed by the nearby single floodlight. We began to discuss the possibility of my using her shots, which I had no intention of looking at, for the article that I had no intention of writing. This, as I was fast learning, was the true goal of serious journalism. Misrepresentation. And pussy.

We began to sidle through the mob into a dark corner in the usual clubland gavotte, leaving the Art to hang out at the bar, so to speak, an island of flesh in a lake of drool.

- So, where do you live?

She asked amiably enough. But I pictured The Earle and shuddered. She looked a bit too clean-cut for the truth. A big problem with The Earle was that I was always leery of admitting that I lived in an actual *septic tank*. I tended to tiptoe around the subject in certain company. So I did a deft little parry by asking where *she* lived. Little Italy, she said. So we talked about Little Italy for a bit, then she repeated the question. Images of radiator-drool and junky corpses danced in front of me. I mumbled something about Washington Square, and she showed more interest. Finally, like a cornered rat, I dropped the iffy name.

- *What?*

She said this backing away.

- Did you say The *Earle* Hotel?
- Um, yeah, but ...
- The *Earle?* Oh my God.
- Yeah, I know. See, it's just while I get myself a better...
- You actually *live* in The Earle Hotel?

She stepped back all the way to the wall, as if to get a better look at me. I might have been a specimen of early swamp fauna in the Natural History Museum. A smile of genuine hilarity lit up her face. You'd have thought she had never heard anything so laughable. She was now openly giggling, looking around as though searching for a wider audience to inform as to my loser status.

- *You live in the Earle Hotel!!*

She shouted this far too loudly. People actually looked over at us.

- I just can't believe this. *I've always wanted to fuck somebody in The Earle Hotel!*

The shit flecks on the wallpaper blossomed into calla lilies. The urine-hued walls gleamed like fields of Tuscan sunflowers through which we gamboled naked and drunk. The relentless giggling and laughter of the boys next door now merely echoed our own, and accompanied us through a long night of horizontal nonsense right through to the morning sleet. We slept all day and strolled out the following sunset into the slush, kicking up the turds and finding it all delightful, there on the corner of Overdose and Bad Posture. I even bought a dime bag of weed without haggling over it and it even turned out to be real pot. My sweet accomplice had chased away every bad vibe from that squalid ant farm and had entirely exorcised the Ghost of Christmas Present. In fact, she *was* my Christmas present. The euphoria lasted a good week. We repeated our foolishness in Little Italy above a restaurant that filled her room with the fragrance of hot pizza. And even when I finally went home, alone, I was still grinning, my damp dump now reminding me only of our foolish pleasure.

I flopped down on my lumpy bed with a big smile and awaited the next-door chamber-music with an almost affectionate anticipation. But apparently there had been a big mood swing next door, in the interim. And it was a turn very much for the worse. Something bad had happened between the two guys while I was away and something very different was going on now. The change was chilling. The relentless hilarity had been replaced by something dark and foreboding. The laughter had turned into a seething row, with rumbled curses from the big guy and staccato outbursts from the little one. All evening long and into the night it went on and it just kept ratcheting up until they were both barking at each other like caged animals. This was much worse than before. I had become almost fond of the goofy bastards, and now it sounded as if actual violence could be in the offing. I feared for the little guy. I was afraid that Woofer might pound Tweeter to a squeaking pulp. He sure sounded big enough.

And at around three in the morning, just as I feared, I was yanked awake by a horrifying sound. The big guy was bellowing like a cornered wildebeest and the wall between us was shuddering under a great pounding noise followed by pitiful little yelps. It sounded like the little guy was being repeatedly flung against the wall. Holy shit! That big thug was trying to *kill* him. I jumped out of bed, ran out of my room and pounded on their door as loud as I could.

The noise inside stopped. The big guy rumbled from inside in a deep bass, "OK, OK. Gimme a minute, will ya?" I gave him a minute. But now I was afraid for my own safety. Why the hell was I standing here without a weapon? The guy sounded huge and who knew what kind of a black rage he was in at this moment, growling like a junkyard dog behind that thin wall. I must be crazy. This was none of my business. This was New Freakin' *York*. Live and let mug. You *don't* interfere. And if the little fella was dead, so what? If you can't kill your own room-mate, whose room-mate *can* you kill? I stepped back as far as I could from the door and angled myself so I could leg it down the stairs if he looked too dangerous. But while I was still dithering, the door was suddenly ripped open so fast I nearly yelped with fright. And I had a good reason to, because, once again, I was utterly unprepared for what greeted me.

He strode slowly and purposefully out into the hallway and turned to face me with his arms at his sides like a deranged gunfighter. He was wearing boxer shorts and one of those white wife-beater tee shirts that psycho killers seem to favor. He addressed me slowly and evenly, staring straight into my eyes without blinking. His voice was deep, very deep, the kind of deep that scares little kids. He said, "It's over, OK? Nobody's hurt, OK? Be cool. Go away. OK? Go to bed." And then he turned slowly, still glowering at me, and shut the door behind himself gently. I stood there, rocking. I could feel myself shaking. I backed away so far that I hit the wall behind me and it spooked me so much that I turned and ran, just *gibbering* with fear, all the way down to the lobby.

It wasn't the deep, deep voice that had freaked me, or the threatening manner, or any of the things he had said. It was simply the sight of the man who had said them. A shortish, fattish, baldish, youngish man. The same man. It was *the same guy. It was the same frigging guy!!!*

Sheeaaaahhh! A loud screech rang out right in front of my face. Holy shit! It was the scraping of the metal bars on the night clerk's cage as he slid it open and stuck his mug out, right into mine.

- What the fuck do *you* want?

- *Want?* What do I *want?* I wanna *move*, man. I wanna get the fuck out of that room! That sonofabitch is *insane*. Certifiable. He should be in a jar at a teaching hospital! Are you kidding me? This lunatic is at *liberty?* Are you *nuts? Lock him up!*

- Calm down, kid, calm down.

Calmly he picked at his teeth with his dirty fingernail.

- You mean that guy next door to you, that, er... talks to hisself?

- *Talks* to himself? My mother *talks* to herself! That whack job is two *entirely different people!* And right now they're *trying to kill each other!*

- OK, OK. Take it easy. Here, have a cigarette. Go ahead, keep the pack. So, er... has he been gettin' a little... outa hand?

- Outa fucking *HAND?!*

- OK, Easy. Go ahead, keep the lighter. I got more back here.

- That man is *criminally* insane. You do *know* that, don't you?

- Oh, yeah, sure. We know. It's the medication, y'see. He gets off it, he gets a little weird.

- A *little* weird?...That whack job is capable of....

- Hey, c'mon. You gotta admit, most of the time he's happy as a lark.

- A figgin' *cuckoo*, more like.

- OK. Look, kid. Calm down. You're a little spooked. Tell you what. Maybe we could give you a little discount? And a promise a good behavior, kinda thing? I'll talk to 'im. He'll listen to me. It's just the medication, y'see. And you *do* have the balcony, you know. That *is* the only one. You *do* got the best room in the joint, kid.

- No. No. No. Forget it. Out of the question.

- Think about it. A little discount.

- No. Absolutely not. Move me. Please. Tomorrow.

I turned and slouched away, totally drained. I dragged my feet to

the elevator with the cigarette shaking between my fingers, thinking about running in and out of my suddenly-terrifying room with
a few things shoved in a bag and legging it down to Little Italy for
a day or two. I pressed the button and waited. The elevator arrived.
The doors opened. I stood there. The doors closed. I stood there.
Then I turned very slowly and walked back, even more slowly, to
the night clerk who was still there, still leaning over the counter
with his head poking through the metal bars looking every bit the
old jailbird that he was, knowing that I would come back. He smiled at
me that old lag's smile and raised one eyebrow ever so slightly in
anticipation of my question, knowing what it would be.

- Er... How *big* of a discount?

EFFING MONKEYS

PANAMA

Everybody loves monkeys, they're so darn cute. Everybody, that is, who has never lived anywhere *near* the filthy, stinking, thieving, lice-infested, masturbating little shits.

It's because of monkeys that I dream I'm naked in public all the time. But I mean, *all the time.* I've dreamt I'm naked in public so consistently for so many years now, that every time I leave my apartment awake, I find myself looking down, you know, *just to check.*

Oh, yes, I know that everybody dreams they're naked in public from time to time. It's normal. The huge difference between my case and, well, *yours* for instance, is that I'm naked in every single dream, and I dream every night. In more than half my dreams I'm naked from the get-go, and in the rest I turn abruptly naked at some point for no logical reason and stay that way for the duration. But the really weird thing is that nobody seems to notice. Nobody ever mentions it. It's expected of me, apparently. And I'm so used to being naked in my dreams that I'm no longer embarrassed by the fact that whatever else is going on, my bare little pointer is pointing at the population. It's a given. And it's never even the *point* of the dream. It's quite incidental to the actual *plot.*

For example, I'm... oh, I don't know... I'm being serenaded by crooning parrots playing Spanish guitars, *while naked.* I'm onstage, flubbing my speech to The Gay Pygmies Association, *while naked.* I am pursued by a melting mob of yellow snowmen, *while naked.* The scenario may change. The package remains in the public domain.

And I don't have to consult Freud to find out why, or spend one cent on a shrink to tell me, either. I know why. It's those effing monkeys.

Don't get me wrong. I've got no beef with Freud, except maybe re that cockeyed Oedipus thing. I mean, kill your dad? O.K. Sure. Fine. But *do* your mother? *Gag* me. Also, since you mention it, I disagree with everything he ever said about women, despite the fact that I *do* love his famous question: *What Does A Woman Want?* What a great book title, ranking right up there with *How To Make A Million Dollars With No Money Down.* What does a women want? This is a very good question and well put. Freud's only mistake, in my opinion, was in *trying to answer it.* There are some questions, like 'My God, why hast thou forsaken me?' or 'Are you out of your *fucking mind?'* that rely for their *entire effect* on remaining unanswered. Where were we?

Oh, yes. I fly in my dreams, too. Naked, of course. And I must say I do fly rather well, if I say so myself. But then I think I drive rather well, too. Others disagree. Often violently. Words like Cavalier, Aggressive, Reckless and 'Stop the frigging car!' are not unheard of among passengers and former friends. During one gentle jaunt through the sun-dappled New England countryside, I was asked with genuine curiosity if we were *being pursued.*

But the naked dream thing is all down to monkeys. In Panama. They stole my clothes and forever changed the course of my dream life. It was on the beach of a little jungle island that I was relieved of my raiment by the smelly, gibbering little penis pullers. At the time, Panama was still barely out of the clutches of the drug-lord dictator Noriega, old pizza-face himself. He was in power so long I always associate Panama with his terrible complexion. Most people, at the mention of Panama think of a big canal. Me, I think of acne. No wonder they never put his face on the money. It looked like a scrotum.

I was there trying to buy an island. Swear to God. There was this little enclave of bite-size islets, entirely formed by mangrove trees, some barely the size of a trailer home, but big enough to build a little piratical, boaty kind of crib on. At the time I could have bought a wee isle for $25,000. Not that I *had* $25,000 at the time. Maybe $25. But the non-existent sum felt at least in the realm of *possibility* via borrowing or theft, and anyway, how often do you get to talk seriously to realtors about your own frickin' *island* with a straight face? And then actually *get shown a few?* "...and over there, sir, you could tie up your yacht." Well, of course.

I was so hot on the idea that I was deep into researching work permits, builders and how to steal $25,000, when I casually asked someone if this endless, interminable rain would quit anytime soon. It had rained since the day I got there, even though it had been all nice balmy sunshine in Panama City for weeks. He looked at me as if I were simple. "Stop? What do you mean, *stop?* It rains here all the time, dude. You didn't know? This is a totally world-famous micro-climate. It's one of the wettest places on the planet. You mean you don't *like it?* Are you *nuts?* It's such a total *trip,* man. And the *mushrooms?*...you can get *sooooooo fucked up!*"

I left the next day and never went back. But during the time I was there, I was given this hot travelers' tip, so I went for one night to this really dreamy resort, not far away but far enough that it wasn't raining. I was splashing a little cash and giving myself a rare treat. And boy was it beautiful. White sands, jungly interior, coconut palms, and nearly the entire long, sunny, white-sand beach all to myself, well, me and a couple of perfect Scandinavian families with perfect tans and perfect children. Oh, and monkeys. So darn cute.

So I wandered off up the old foamy strand to get far enough away from the flawless Swedes that I could take off the swimming trunks and brown the white bits. Real bliss. In and out of the water, tanning and swimming, swimming and tanning. Heaven. And occasionally I would glance over at the cute little monkeys in the distance doing their usual cute little monkey things – picking their noses, eating each other's lice and ticks, sniffing each other's assholes, jerking off and shagging their mothers and sisters. Oh, you didn't *know?*

Finally as the afternoon wore on I went for a long walk away from my filthy, incestuous, lice-riddled, jibbering distant cousins, leaving my one tiny garment on the sand next to my bottle of water. It was a rather bright, lurid little Speedo number with orchids or some such blossoms plastered all over it in neon colors. But in the best possible taste, of course.

I was gone quite a while. Being naked just felt wildly reckless and a bit naughty, to be frank. I could never get over the total kiddie thrill of it, just to stride along shamelessly and rock out with the cock out. So I had already wandered a good kilometer away from everybody in this foolish Adam and Eve fashion when I started to feel the chill of the falling sun and the rising breeze on my reddening rump, and reluctantly turned back, taking my own sweet time. And when I got back to my spot, to re-climb into my fashionable item, my fashionable item was no longer there. Well, of course.

And, of course, in the distance, the monkeys, so darn cute, were having a major uproar among themselves, fighting murderously with their mothers and sisters over a small but very lurid piece of cloth printed with orchids or some such blossoms. But in the best possible taste.

Have you ever tried to retrieve something a monkey has ripped off? Don't bother. There are places in Bali where the little bastards wander over to you and you take their photograph and they're so darn cute, aren't they? Then they *lunge at you* and rip your camera off your neck and your hat off your head and your glasses off your face and run off with them. God help you if you were wearing a toupé. And if you run after them, that's when they really show you exactly how far they've evolved away from your sorry ass in the area of velocity, agility, dexterity, balance and cheek. You're toast, you flat-footed lard bag. And if you really race after them, they're up a tree faster than a rat up a drainpipe, already rogering their mothers and jerking off all over you while you're still standing there panting and coughing, half blind from your no-glasses and out many hundreds of dollars depending on the price of the camera. Or the rug.

So, hey now. The monkeys have stolen my lurid loincloth, my only item of clothing and modesty, and there's nothing I can do about it. That's that. I'm totally bare-ass naked and there in the distance between me and my bijou seafront special-treat junior villa are - oh what a lovely coincidence - every one of those perfect-featured blond Scandinaves with all their perfect-featured blond babes and sucklings. They're all now gathered around a lovely big sunset bonfire and barbecue, all laughing and joking and milling around, and all about to get a load of my pink paraphernalia.

And at that particular point on the beach, now at high tide, the distance between villas and water has become a very narrow strip of sandy beach. So to get to my Superior Junior villa, I have to walk not just *past* all of them, I have to walk *through and among* all of them. Naked. Oh joy.

Well, ask yourself. What would *you* do? I could have swum in a long loop around them all if I were more Tarzanic, but I'm not much of a swimmer and the current there was a bit stiff. And anyway, I didn't do that, so it's moot. No. I decided to sort of clown my way through the embarrassment by covering myself with a huge leaf that I had spotted at the top of the beach where the previous tide had thrown up a few odd bits of flotsam, and then to do a sort of Gypsy Rose Lee fan-dance through the whole throng, turn it all into a bit of a joke, be the life and soul of the party sort of thing, while retaining my modesty and covering up my private parts the whole time.

I couldn't just brass it out and march though them with it all out there gleaming, because there were little girls there, you see. I had to cover myself or be a pervert. And it didn't really matter if the little girls saw my bottom. That's not the bit that might slightly traumatize them if they hadn't seen a grown man's haberdashery before, and there was a good chance that these ones hadn't, even with their being suave Swedes and all, because I noticed that the women were not topless and the tots were not tottering around bottomless. So, they weren't the type of willy-wagging titty-touting Teutons you see on the Greek islands, brandishing their rude bits at you. And so my plan seemed *very thoughtful* on my part, well figured out, plus a bit of a lark for the whole family, a show, fun for the kids, a silly chap doing a silly dance on the beach. Well, this was the plan, anyway. And it seemed like such a good idea. *At the time.*

Philodendron: the botanical term. *Elephant Ear*: the common name. That's what this giant leaf was. You've seen them in conservatories and in Tarzan movies. Huge, wide, and nearly a meter long, with big fat stems, and this one was a huge specimen. I always imagine them being wielded by stylish goblins, using them as fans to cool some giant psychedelic caterpillar in a turban, in some arty-farty fantasy flick, don't you? You don't? Oh, please yourself.

Anyway, when I picked this huge thing up from among the tide-line jetsam I was amazed by how feathery light it was for its size. This was because it was dead and pickled in brine. It was not a fat, flexible green one, but a stiff, dried-out one, tanned to a nice coppery brown, quite beautiful actually, leathery and brittle, a real crusader-sized shield for my groin. I tapped it hard a few times to test its structural integrity, and it seemed pretty tough and strong to me for a dead leaf. Rock hard. I thought I might even try and fly it home to my place and stick it on the wall as a poetic reminder of a goofy moment. All in all it was perfect, a sort of jungle antique, an object of beauty that would add a certain aesthetic *oomph* to my coming buffoonery. I started to quite look forward to my little lounge act on the beach for my small, select and very attractive audience. One night only. By invitation, sort of thing.

So off I launched towards stardom, loping along the beach, practicing a few moves - a wiggle, a dip, a bump, a grind - you know the sort of thing. All that goofy striptease shit beloved of pole-dancers everywhere. Well, if you don't, you should get out more.

And so far, nobody seemed to have noticed me approaching, getting closer, a tallish man with a big brown leaf down to his knees, wiggling and strutting like a total fricking lunatic, to be brutally frank. Luckily, my audience had all moved towards the water's edge where they were now eating their hotdogs and paddling in the sunset. Great. So now I could turn my bare bottom entirely away from them through this critical narrow passage and not even have *that* visible. It was all working out even better than I'd planned. So I approached the group facing them, practising my goofy little fan dance, presenting them all with my very big, very modest leaf. Perfect. I was very close now, within only a few yards, but I was totally covered. They could all have a good laugh without even knowing I was entirely naked behind the big copper shield. This really was a great idea!

When they noticed me for the first time, I was already right there, in among them. They all nudged each other and all turned to watch me at the same moment, stepping back a little, it seemed, as if a quite shocked. That's odd, I thought. Oh, well. *Showtime!*

I let 'em have it, the full Vegas. I bumped and grinded with maximum wallop, waving my free arm over my head, doing the dip, the bump, the grind, the whole nutty stripper menu. I was having a great time. I *killed.* Well I thought I did. Until... I noticed...that...the reaction was not at all what I had expected. Totally the opposite, in fact. There were no cheers and applause and laughter. None. Nothing. I was bombing. I was an absolute total dud. There was just a sort of shocked silence, with a seriously strong overtone of grave disapproval. Oh, dear. What a humorless lot. I must have chosen the squarest bunch of Euro fuddy-duddies ever assembled. One mother was actually covering the eyes of her little girl toddler, while shaking her head at me in a most disapproving tut-tut sort of way. Two older girls were standing there, holding hands, pointing and staring at my leaf, eyes wide, giggling nervously. Two of the dads had their hands on their hips, unsmiling, almost threatening in their body language. I felt quite nervous all of a sudden. Had I so seriously miscalculated my reception that I was in danger of being possibly attacked, even? Yikes. Well, *excuuuuse me* for trying to amuse you, you dour Danes. I'll just go home and shoot myself, shall I? What a lousy, dull bunch of bastards. Jesus!

I stopped gyrating and stumped off towards my villa, turning my big leaf around to cover my ass modestly as I disappeared. But then I stood on my doorstep and, placing it in front of me again, I turned around theatrically and did one last big bump and grind of annoyance, opened my door, walked into my place and saw myself in the big floor-length mirror for the first time, exactly as they had all just seen me, with my big leaf held in front of me.

Ooooh! Oh, God! Oh, no! Oh, *great buckets of steaming shit!!!*

At what exact point *the entire massive center of the leaf had fallen away,* I don't know. It doesn't really matter, does it?

Let's just assume, since the reaction was so utter and total, that it had fallen off long before I had arrived at the, ahem, Performance Area. So, not only had I wiggled and waggled and waved my totally visible ass-handle at everyone from infant to grandma and from just a few feet away, I had also been holding a big, bright copper-colored leaf-shaped *empty frame* to bring *extra attention* to the wiggling, waggling and waving, in case anyone had failed to notice. *As if.*

There was a banging on my front door. A very loud, enraged male parental banging. I ran naked out the back door, hid in the jungle, and stayed there for a very long time.

And now I'm naked in every dream. And I dream every night.

If you enjoyed this collection of travel memoirs,
or would like to comment on any of them,
or for additional material in the same vein,
or to contribute your own foolish stories,
or if you have nothing better to do and
maybe it's raining outside, please visit
www.foreignfool.com

37374645R00157

Made in the USA
Middletown, DE
26 November 2016